Total Forgiveness

Also by R. T. Kendall

The Anointing – Yesterday, Today, Tomorrow
The Gift of Giving
The Sensitivity of the Spirit
The Thorn in the Flesh
Worshipping God

Compiled by Louise and R. T. Kendall

Great Christian Prayers

Total Forgiveness

Achieving God's Greatest Challenge

R. T. Kendall

Hodder & Stoughton
LONDON SYDNEY AUCKLAND

British Library Cataloguing in Publication Data
A record for this book is available from the British Library

ISBN 0 340 75639 X

Typeset by Avon Dataset Ltd, Bidford-on-Avon, Warks

Printed and bound in Great Britain by
Clays Ltd, St Ives plc

The paper and board used in this paperback are natural recyclable
products made from wood grown in sustainable forests.
The manufacturing processes conform to the environmental
regulations of the country of origin.

Hodder & Stoughton
A Division of Hodder Headline Ltd
338 Euston Road
London NW1 3BH
www.madaboutbooks.com

To Melissa

Contents

Foreword

One of the greatest subjects of the Third Millennium will be the relationship between the developed industrialised countries of the West and the developing countries in the Third World, especially in Africa.

A new world order has emerged which requires global mediation – a mediation whose main objective would be to contribute to the solution of the relatively new area of ethnic conflicts within nations as well as conflicts between nations, and also to contribute to the promotion of world and in particular African economic growth, development and welfare. Some of us who have been involved in the practical mediation of these conflicts have come to the stark realisation that nations need to *forgive* each other for their past exploitation and suppression of their weaker neighbours just as much as individuals need to do. For a people who have been so traumatised by the ravages of the Cold War and colonialism – a people who are seeking to come to terms with their history of oppression, conflict and disagreement; a people who are just scraping the rock bottom of despair and despondency as the people of Africa are doing – *there can be no future without forgiveness*.

It is in this context that I have found Dr R. T. Kendall's book *Total Forgiveness* to be immensely timely and appropriate at this particular juncture in our human history. It is a book which should be read by every race and nation in the world. As much as the Africans and other races need to forgive each other for the atrocities they have inflicted on their neighbours in the name of politically-determined ethnic conflicts and religion – such as happened in Rwanda, Bosnia-Herzegovina and Kosovo and Northern Ireland, and is continuing to happen in Sierra Leone, Sudan, Angola, Liberia, Guinea, Somalia, the Ethiopian–Eritrean conflict, Algeria and the Democratic Republic of the Congo, to mention only a few – there is also a lot of forgiveness to be undertaken between Europe, America and the Arab world on the one hand and Africa on the other. The people from these nations were involved, through the Atlantic and Arabian slave trade in Africa, in what was the largest intercontinental forced migration of wageless labour from one society to another, a development which followed purely racial lines. This was followed by the European Scramble for Africa between 1884 and 1914, which has been described as the greatest land-grab in history. That is why Africans, and to a certain extent Asians and Latin Americans, are hurting and bitter when they look back at their history and what was done to them by the other races. Looking back at past history is important because without a knowledge of history and one's links to the past, humankind is a social amnesiac, intellectually and therefore to some extent emotionally rootless. Also, as the great

American philosopher George Santayana once said, those who cannot remember the past are condemned to repeat it.

But R. T. Kendall has taught us, through this book, that bitterness, however justified, will just consume our souls and achieve nothing. We must, therefore, learn to forgive even if we don't forget. Nelson Mandela is perhaps the best example in the twentieth century of a man who has taught us how to forgive. After twenty-seven years of political incarceration – the longest-serving political prisoner in the world – he emerged unscathed and told his people to forgive their former white oppressors and instead fix their attention on the future: on building a new united nation. In spite of the devastating trauma of apartheid, Mandela chose the path of forgiveness and reconciliation rather than the policy of revenge and vindictiveness. The world had expected that the most ghastly bloodbath would overwhelm South Africa. This did not happen. Then the world thought that once a democratically-elected government was in place with Mandela installed as its first black President, those who for so long had been denied their rights – whose dignity had been trodden underfoot, callously and without compunction – would go on the rampage, unleashing an orgy of revenge and retribution that would devastate their common motherland. But this did not happen either. South Africans managed an extraordinary, reasonably peaceful transition from the awfulness of repression to the relative stability of a non-racial democratic political dispensation. They had perhaps surprised even themselves at first by how much equanimity they had shown as some of the gory details of the past were rehearsed later in the Truth and Reconciliation Commission. It was a phenomenon that the world could not dismiss as insignificant. I am grateful to God who enabled me to play a role in that reconciliation and forgiving process, which saw the holding of peaceful and democratic elections in April 1994 and the avoidance of a major ethnic and racial war.

The Arab–Israeli conflict has gone on for such a long time because it is unfortunately based on the policy of massive and instant mutual retaliation – the policy of a tooth for a tooth and an eye for an eye. But, in the final analysis, the parties to this terrible conflict will have to sit round a table, on the basis of give and take, and negotiate a peaceful and lasting agreement. This must be based on the policy of reconciliation, forgiveness and restorative justice and not retributive justice.

Clearly, the world has been waiting for just such a book as this and R. T. Kendall has done humanity a great service.

PROFESSOR WASHINGTON A. J. OKUMU

NAIROBI

I FEBRUARY 2001

Preface

Every author probably thinks that his or her latest book is one's best or most important so far. And I certainly do think that about this one. It is by far the book that has the greatest potential to heal the human heart of any that I have written. I do pray that this book will exceed all expectations for every person who reads what follows. It is designed to set one free.

I want to thank Rob Parsons, Julia Fisher, Susan Perlman, Michael Schluter and Lyndon Bowring for reading the manuscript. These friends have been an incalculable encouragement to me by their pertinent suggestions and loving support. My thanks to Sheila Penton who typed the manuscript and to David Moloney, my editor at Hodder, for his patience and help.

Most of all, I thank Professor Washington Okumu of Nairobi, Kenya, for his willingness to write the Foreword. A student of Harvard and Cambridge, Professor Okumu studied under Dr Henry Kissinger, among others, at Harvard

University. They later became friends and worked together to bring about peace and reconciliation in South Africa. Professor Okumu's greatest legacy is that he was able to bring former President De Klerk of South Africa, Chief Mangosuthu Buthelezi and Nelson Mandela together and brokered peace among them when Dr Kissinger and Lord Carrington had failed to do so. This was one of the great miracles of the twentieth century. The result was that Nelson Mandela became the first black President of South Africa and all the world is grateful. Parallel with that event was that Professor Okumu was almost certainly the main force responsible for averting a civil war in South Africa.

This book is lovingly dedicated to my daughter Melissa. She knows what it is to suffer deep hurts but also what it means to forgive – totally.

R. T. KENDALL
WESTMINSTER CHAPEL, LONDON
I FEBRUARY 2001

Introduction

> R.T., you must totally forgive them. Until you totally forgive them you will be in chains. Release them and you will be released.

Nobody had ever talked to me like that in my life. These words, given to me unexpectedly by my friend Josif Tson of Romania, are among the most important words anybody has ever personally shared with me. 'Faithful are the wounds of a friend' (Prov. 27:6).

In the 5 June 2000 issue of London's *Daily Express* there appeared an article with this headline: 'Can you learn to forgive?' The opening words were these: 'Bearing a grudge can hold you back and even damage your health.' The writer of the article, Susan Pape, had interviewed Dr Ken Hart, lecturer at Leeds University, who had been running the 'world's first forgiveness course', designed to help people forgive their enemies and let go of grudges. Participants ranged from victims of burglary, to jilted husbands, to those who have been bullied. All had one thing in common: they were angry, bitter, and wanted revenge.

This was not, as far as I know, a Christian course; it would seem that this was a case of people doing something biblical without knowing it. There are indications that the world is starting to recognise the merit of forgiving people and it may be that it is Christians who are lagging behind. Sadly, for too long this included me.

Most of us have times in our lives when we are pushed to the limit in terms of forgiveness. I remember what happened to me with such clarity. I have vowed not to re-tell the story, but suffice it to say that I had never before been hurt so deeply. The wrong that I believe was done to me hit just about every area of my life: my family, my ministry, my very sense of self-worth. I felt at times like Job: 'I have no peace, no quietness; I have no rest, but only turmoil' (Job 3:26). I felt like David: 'Answer me quickly, O LORD; my spirit faints with longing. Do not hide your face from me or I will be like those who go down to the pit' (Ps. 143:7). I doubt whether those who brought this upon me had any idea what I went through and I pray with all my heart they never will.

I blush to admit that those words above from Josif Tson were spoken to me since I became minister of Westminster Chapel. I, if anyone, should not have needed such a word. Nobody should have to tell a mature minister of the gospel of Christ the most obvious and fundamental teaching of the New Testament. Here I was in the ministry of our Lord Jesus Christ, but filled with so much hurt and bitterness that I can only say I did not deserve to be there. That is why I am almost ashamed to confess this. But I tell it for two reasons: (1) it shows how gracious God has been to me in spite of my anger and self-pity, and (2) it might encourage you.

What is possibly even more astonishing is that prior to this my unforgiving spirit had not bothered me all that much. If you had reminded me of Jesus' words that we should 'love one another' (John 13:35) or of that petition in the Lord's Prayer, 'Forgive us our trespasses as we forgive those who have trespassed against us', I would have replied, '*Of course* I know about that.' I probably assumed that since nobody is perfect and because we all sin in some measure every day, that this sort of sin (bitterness) surely fell into that category. Moreover, God fully understood and sympathised with *my* particular circumstances, which were – I thought – unusual. In other words, I rationalised my attitude and behaviour.

But, mercifully, the power of the Holy Spirit came that day with Josif's words to me. And yet I was angry; I was hemmed in. Josif's words were pivotal for me in the end, though, and life-changing. I was never to be the same again.

To be honest, I only told him of my problem because I thought I would get a bit of sympathy from a man I deeply respected and thought would be on my side. I expected him to put his arm on my shoulder and say, 'R.T., you are right to feel as angry as you do. Get it out of your system.' But no. He compassionately but soberly rebuked me and would not let me off the hook.

Those words came to me during the greatest trial I had ever experienced up until then. I had not felt able to tell anybody at all about it, but because Josif was from Romania and would never tell, I told him everything. 'Is there anything more?' he asked. 'No, that's it,' I said. Then came those remarkable words, in his lovely Romanian accent: 'You must totally forgive them.'

'I can't,' I replied.

'You can and you must,' he insisted.

'I've just remembered. There is more. What I didn't tell you . . .'

'R.T.,' he interrupted, 'you must totally forgive them. Release them and you will be set free.'

It was the hardest thing I had ever been asked to do.

I am not telling you that this is plain sailing. What I write about in this book is far easier said than done. I repeat, it was the hardest thing I had ever been asked to do, but it was also the greatest thing I had ever been asked to do.

An unexpected blessing emerged as I began to forgive: a peace came into my heart that I hadn't felt in years. It was wonderful; I had forgotten what it was like. It had come to me years before – on 31 October 1955, when driving my car one Monday morning from my church in Palmer, Tennessee. Readers of *The Anointing* (Hodder & Stoughton, 1998) and *The Sensitivity of the Spirit* (Hodder & Stoughton, 2000) may recall some of the story. I was on my way back from my student pastorate to Trevecca Nazarene College in Nashville. As I drove, there was the Lord Jesus literally interceding for me at the right hand of the Father. I have never felt so loved. Jesus was praying for me with all his heart. The next thing I remember – an hour later – was hearing Jesus say to the Father, 'He wants it.' I heard the Father's voice reply, 'He can have it.' At that moment it was like liquid fire entering my chest. I remembered John Wesley's words: 'I felt my heart strangely warmed.' I felt an incredible peace, one that is not really possible to describe. The person of Jesus was more real to me than anything or anyone around me. This lasted for several months, but eventually the feeling faded.

Now, though, it was beginning to come back – the peace and the sense of Jesus' nearness. All because I was setting those people free, forgiving them; letting them off the hook.

However, as I found myself once again thinking about 'what they did' I would get churned up inside. I would say to myself, 'Those people are going to get away with this. This is not fair. They won't get caught. They won't be found out. Nobody will know. This is not right.' And that sweet peace left again.

I therefore noticed an interesting cycle: when I felt the spirit of total forgiveness towards those who had wrongd me, the peace would return; when I dwelt with resentment on the likelihood that they wouldn't get caught, the peace would leave.

I had to make an important decision: which do I prefer – the peace or the bitterness? I couldn't have it both ways. I began to see that *I* was the great loser – the impoverished one – by not forgiving. My bitterness wasn't damaging anyone but myself.

When we are bitter we delude ourselves into thinking that those who hurt us are more likely to be punished as long as we are set on revenge. We are afraid to let go of the feelings of revenge. After all, if we don't make plans to see that justice is done, how will justice be done? We make ourselves believe that it is up to us to step in.

This is a lie – the devil's lie: 'Do not take revenge, my friends, but leave room for God's wrath, for it is written: "It is mine to avenge; I will repay," says the Lord' (Rom. 12:19). We only hurt ourselves when we dwell on what has happened to us and fantasise about what it will be like when 'they' get punished. Most of all, we grieve the Holy Spirit of God. This is why we lose that inner peace.

I have come to the conclusion that the chief way we grieve the Spirit is by bitterness. The main reason I say this is because it is the first thing the apostle Paul says immediately after warning us not to grieve the Spirit:

And do not grieve the Holy Spirit of God, with whom you were sealed for the day of redemption. Get rid of all bitterness, rage and anger, brawling and slander, along with every form of malice. Be kind and compassionate to one another, forgiving each other, just as in Christ God forgave you. (Ephesians 4:30–2)

It is also my own experience that the quickest way I seem to lose inner peace is when I allow bitterness to re-enter my heart. It is then that the peace leaves. It's not worth it!

I made a decision for inner peace, but I found that I had to carry out that decision by a *daily* commitment to forgive those who had hurt me, and to forgive them totally. I therefore let them utterly off the hook and resigned myself to the knowledge that: (1) they wouldn't get caught or found out; (2) nobody would ever know what they did; and (3) they would prosper and be blessed as though they had done no wrong. What is more, I actually willed this! I prayed for this! I asked God to forgive them. But I have had to do it every day in order to *keep* the peace within my heart. Having been on both sides, I can tell you: the peace is better. The bitterness isn't worth it.

I write this book to encourage anyone who has had a problem with forgiving people. I write this in order for such people to see the real reasons to forgive. Therefore I write this to help anyone who has been hurt, however deeply, to learn how to forgive. Many will have been through far worse experiences than anything I have been through, but I have come to believe that the only way forward is through total forgiveness – whatever the experience. I want this book to change lives in the same way that my own was changed by Josif's loving rebuke to me.

I am convinced that this theme of total forgiveness is perhaps more crucially needed at this present moment than nearly any other teaching in the Bible.

The reasons I say this are as follows. First, whenever I go and preach the message of total forgiveness, there is a most tremendous response. No sermon or theme I touch on comes even close to the chord that is struck when I get on to this subject. It therefore tells me that there is a terrific need out there – even among Christians – to come to grips with this matter.

Secondly, when I return to this theme in my own church, as I often do, even though it may have been mentioned only a few weeks before, it is usually as though I have never said it! Clearly, this matter of getting rid of bitterness and totally forgiving one another is not easily dealt with. I sometimes wonder if it would be good if I preached on it every week!

Thirdly, it is evident that I never felt sufficiently bothered by my own failure to deal with forgiving people who had let me down. Why? I have asked this question many times. I surely knew that this was Jesus' message, so why was I not gripped by this? Why did I need to hear this from a man who lived behind the Iron Curtain (as we used to call it)? Did the Christians in Eastern Europe have an emphasis that we in the West took for granted?

Why hadn't I been confronted by this message of total forgiveness by all of my heroes – both living and dead? I have read hundreds of sermons by the Puritans and the Reformers, yet I cannot recall being told by them that I must totally forgive or otherwise grieve the Holy Spirit. Godly though my own parents were, I can't say that total forgiveness was something I was consciously taught at home. Not a single mentor (that I can recall) emphasised this as a lifestyle. On the contrary, I seem to remember being told: 'Treat them with contempt', 'Distance yourself from them', 'Give them a cold shoulder', 'Teach them a lesson', 'They must be punished' – or words to that effect.

Fourthly, it may be cold comfort to learn that a growing number of informed people have recently discerned this incredible neglect. In a recent issue of *Christianity Today* (10 January 2000), with the bold words 'The Forgiveness Factor' on the front cover, writer Gary Thomson writes that this teaching has been greatly overlooked. Theologian Lewis Smedes was one of the first to emphasise this – in 1984! Professor Robert Enright, President of the International Forgiveness Institute, who describes himself as an 'evangelical Catholic', has commented that prior to Lewis Smedes's *Forgive and Forget* (Harper San Francisco, 1984): 'If you collected every theological book about person-to-person forgiveness [as opposed to divine-human forgiveness], you could hold them all in one hand.' If this is true, although it doesn't excuse me, it would help to explain my own lack of awareness of this theme – and the reason I wasn't truly taught it.

Some people understandably marvel if a particular doctrine so obvious in Scripture could apparently lie dormant for so many hundreds of years. But when one thinks about the plain teaching of forgiving one another, and how this has managed to be swept under the carpet for so long, it should cause many of us who are church leaders to repent together. Furthermore, had this teaching become the emphasis and lifestyle of all those of us who are in some measure of authority, there would possibly not have been the division and hurt that has characterised many Christians. Sadly, the present age is no different from that of any other in church history in that it has been characterised by fellow believers speaking and writing against one another. This is often disguised as a doctrinal battle for truth, but so often the veneer is paper-thin and underneath are the age-old jealousies, petty agendas and sheer humanness that affect us all.

Fifthly, social scientists are discovering that forgiveness may help lead to victims' emotional health – and even physical healing and wholeness. As recently as the early 1980s, Dr Glen Hamden went to the University of Kansas library and looked up the word 'forgiveness' in *Psychological Abstracts*; he couldn't find a single reference. But things are changing. Former President Jimmy Carter, Archbishop Desmond Tutu, and former missionary Elisabeth Elliot have been leading a $10million 'Campaign for Forgiveness Research', established as a non-profit corporation to attract donations that will support forgiveness research proposals. In 1998 the John Templeton Foundation awarded research grants for the study of forgiveness to twenty-nine scholars. One of the main discoveries was that the first person who gains from forgiveness is the person who does the forgiving. But should this surprise us?

And yet this book is wholly about *biblical* teaching not the results of psychological or sociological research. I want to show what Jesus taught and how this was interpreted by the apostles. The benefits of this book may certainly have positive psychological or even physical benefits, but I am going to centre on the *spiritual blessing* that comes to those who take Jesus' teaching of total forgiveness seriously. In a word: it is about receiving a greater anointing.

Because forgiving those who have hurt us severely can be very difficult to experience, especially when trust is shattered, Michelle Nelson has chosen to speak of degrees or different types of forgiveness. She has listed three categories: 1 *Detached forgiveness*. This is when there is a reduction in negative feelings towards the offender, but no reconciliation has taken place. 2 *Limited forgiveness*. This means a reduction in negative feelings towards the offender, and partial relationship is restored with them. There is also a decrease in the emotional intensity in the relationship. 3 *Full forgiveness*. This means a total cessation of negative feelings towards the offender, and the relationship is restored and grows.

I have chosen to speak of 'total' forgiveness (if only because that is the expression my friend Josif Tson used with me), but this book is also about total forgiveness *even when there is not a restoration of a relationship*. One must totally forgive those who will not be reconciled. This therefore refers to what we do in our *hearts*. If there is no reconciliation, then there can still be total forgiveness. This therefore applies even to someone who must still totally forgive those who are not now alive. It must happen in the heart. If it happens there, peace emerges – with or without a complete restoration in the relationship. What matters is that the Holy Spirit dwells in us *ungrieved*. This means that the Spirit is utterly himself, as I try to show in *The Sensitivity of the Spirit*. The degree to which the Holy Spirit is himself in me will be the degree to which I am like Jesus and carry out his teachings.

1

What is total forgiveness?

We all have a story to tell. You who read these lines may think it is impossible to forgive an unfaithful husband or wife. You may feel you cannot forgive the abusive parent. You may feel you cannot forgive something that has been done to your son or daughter. How can we forgive the church leader who took advantage of his position? What about the person who lied to us or about us, only to be believed by many? There is the rapist out there. The child abuser. The relative who abused. The racist. The thief. The former close friend who is now an enemy. The list is endless.

Forgiving those who have hurt our loved ones

I received a heart-rending letter from someone who had heard me preach on 'total forgiveness' a few years ago. They told me what their son-in-law had done to their daughter and grand-children. It was awful. 'Are you saying we must totally forgive our son-in-law?' they asked. That was a hard one. But I had to

11

write back: yes. I wished I could carry the letter to them by hand and then be there when they read it. My heart went out to them. I have received not a few other letters that have described everything from infidelity to incest to rape to brutal lying. It is enough to make me look very deeply indeed into what I preach – and what I write in this book.

The hardest matter I have had to face in recent years is not the matter I talked to Josif Tson about. That episode now looks like a picnic compared to what I have faced since. One of my greatest struggles has been seeing one of our family hurt by Christians. I find it much, much easier to forgive what people have done or said regarding me personally than what pertains to my children.

It is not unlike Corrie ten Boom having to forgive the prison guard who was so cruel to her sister. Corrie saw this man treat her sister – who died shortly afterwards – extremely viciously when both of them were in prison for protecting Jews in Holland during the Second World War. Years later, Corrie was seated on the platform, preparing to give her talk, when she spotted this very man in the congregation. She struggled in her heart. She prayed in desperation for God to fill her heart with the love of Jesus. He did, but the matter wasn't any easier when, after the service, this guard rather glibly said, in so many words, how good God is to forgive all of us. She wondered how sorry he really was.

It is often easier, then, it seems to me, to forgive what is done to us personally than what is done to those close to us. But it is still very, very hard to forgive those who have hurt us directly, especially when they feel not the slightest twinge of conscience. When we can see they are sorry it makes it a lot easier.

But no one seemed very sorry at the cross of Jesus. There

was no justice at his 'trial' – if you could call it that. There was glee in the faces of the people who got what they wanted: ' "Crucify him!" they shouted' (Mark 15:13). Furthermore, 'Those who passed by hurled insults at him, shaking their heads and saying, "So! You who are going to destroy the temple and build it in three days, come down from the cross and save yourself!" ' (Mark 15:29–30.) They shouted, 'Let this Christ, this King of Israel, come down now from the cross, that we may see and believe' (Mark 15:32). And what was Jesus' response? 'Father, forgive them, for they do not know what they are doing' (Luke 23:34). It must be our response as well.

He might have said, 'I forgive you', but such words would have been misinterpreted and wasted. It would also have been casting his pearls before pigs (Matt. 7:6). Instead, Jesus asked the *Father* to forgive them. That was a far grander gesture in any case. By asking the Father to forgive them it showed *he* had forgiven them; he released all of them from their guilt. He likewise set the Father free from having to punish them by asking him not to take revenge on them. It was not a perfunctory prayer; Jesus meant it. And it was gloriously answered! They were among the very ones Peter addressed on the Day of Pentecost (Acts 2:14–41) and who were converted.

The ultimate proof of total forgiveness

The ultimate proof of total forgiveness is when we sincerely petition the Father to let off the hook those who have hurt us – even if they have hurt those close to us.

At the height of one of the fiercest eras at Westminster Chapel in the 1980s I had to come face to face with this. I recalled Josif Tson's words to me, so I prayed for certain people to be forgiven. I felt nothing; I just said it. But then, after a few moments, it was as though the Lord said to me: 'Do you know what you are asking me to do?' I thought that I knew. So I said, 'Yes.' He then seemed to reply, 'Are you now asking me to set them free as if they had done nothing?' That sobered me. I needed some time on that one. But while I was pondering that, it seemed that the Lord reminded me of what he had forgiven *me* of. I was frightened of the thought that he might reveal – or let come out – some things for which he had forgiven me. I then humbly prayed, 'Yes, Lord, I ask you to forgive them.' He then seemed to say, 'Do you therefore mean that I should bless them and prosper them?' Once more I needed a little time. Then the Lord seemed to say, 'What if I forgive and bless you, R.T., in proportion to how you want me to forgive and bless them?' By this time I had no choice, neither could I claim any great piety on my part for forgiving them and praying that they be blessed. God had boxed me into a corner and I surrendered. By this time I sincerely and truly prayed for them to be forgiven and blessed as though they had done no offence, but I cannot claim that my prayer was particularly godly or unselfish.

Some time ago there was a television series depicting Christians who had forgiven those who had hurt them. The producer, not a Christian, was profoundly moved. He said that while he could take or leave preaching, he could not ignore this. 'Something must be happening in their lives,' he said. He added: it is so 'unnatural' for a person to forgive those who have hurt them and to desire reconciliation. In a word: there is no greater testimony to the lost than this. But this is, after all, the message of the New Testament: 'that God was reconciling the world to himself in Christ, not counting men's sins against them. And he has committed to us the message of reconciliation' (2 Cor. 5:19). 'But God demonstrates his own love for us in this: While we were still sinners, Christ died for us' (Rom. 5:8).

I once addressed a group of missionaries in the south of France. I was given hospitality in a home while there by one who had been a Muslim but was now a Christian missionary. I was astonished at this and marvelled at his change of life. He told me he had been led to Christ by some British soldiers when he lived in Madagascar. But what I really wanted to know was what actually won him over: 'What argument did they use? What line of reasoning persuaded you to turn from Islam to Christianity?' He replied: 'It wasn't what they said; it was *them*.' This really challenged me. It made me see the folly of imagining we are only going to win people over by superior arguments, or by great preaching. What impresses the world most, I have to say, is *changed lives* – for which there is no natural explanation.

The motivation to forgive can have a natural explanation

The television producer mentioned above called reconciliation and forgiving one another 'unnatural', but that is not quite true. The motivation to forgive often has a natural explanation. For Jesus speaks to us in a way that gets our attention – if only by appealing to our self-interest.' "Do not judge, or you too will be judged" ' (Matt. 7:1). A motive for not judging others is to stop ourselves from being judged. If a person's chief desire is for a greater anointing, and he is told that this anointing will come in proportion to the degree that he forgives others, then he is more motivated to forgive. I for one want a greater anointing. If you could have read my heart

15

of hearts when Josif Tson counselled me, 'You must totally forgive them', I suspect you would have discovered that – at bottom – I acquiesced because I wanted more blessing from God. Therefore it is not entirely 'unnatural' that one tries to forgive.

For example, I unexpectedly saw a person in one of our services who had severely hurt one of our children. It was just before I was scheduled to preach. I felt like Corrie ten Boom must have felt. In a flash the Lord seemed to say to me: 'You say you want Revival in this church. What if Revival hinges on whether you totally forgive this person?' I felt awful. I felt selfish. I felt trapped. But I had to make a decision on the spot – at least it felt that way – as to whether I really wanted Revival in our church. In other words, which meant more to me: getting even with one who had hurt one of our children or the blessing of the Spirit? I opted for the latter, but my prayer still had a natural explanation. I did not want it on my conscience that I was obstructing the blessing of the Spirit when all around me there were those who were earnestly praying for this. I still struggle in this area and think – just maybe – I have totally forgiven this person. I have asked the Lord to bless this person and let them off the hook, but it hasn't been easy. Totally forgiving somebody doesn't necessarily mean we will want to go on holiday with them.

Our mandate is to forgive

Our mandate is to forgive as we have been forgiven: 'Be kind and compassionate to one another, forgiving each other, just as in Christ God forgave you' (Eph. 4:32); 'Bear with each other and forgive whatever grievances you may have against one another. Forgive as the Lord forgave you' (Col. 3:13).

I therefore ask, how has the Lord forgiven me? Answer: my sins, which are many, will never be held against me and nobody will know what I have done. 'As far as the east is from the west, so far has he removed our transgressions from us' (Ps. 103:12). It therefore follows that I will not hold people responsible for what they have done to me. I will hold nothing against them and I will tell nobody what they have done.

You might reply: 'But you told everything to Josif Tson.' True – and I'm so glad that I did. But I wasn't planning to start a smear campaign against anybody. Certainly my attitude was not perfect – I wanted a lot of sympathy, but I was mercifully put in my place by Josif. Had it not been this way, I am not sure how long I would have kept quiet. I can only thank God that he sent this wise person before I might have destroyed myself.

David must have felt like this. In those years before he was made king – when he was 'tomorrow's man' in a time of preparation (see my book *The Anointing*) – he was eager to get vengeance on Nabal. But God sent Abigail – in the nick of time – who appealed to David's common sense:

David said to Abigail, 'Praise be to the LORD, the God of Israel, who has sent you today to meet me. May you be blessed for your good judgment and for keeping me from bloodshed this day and from avenging myself with my own hands. Otherwise, as surely as the LORD, the God of Israel, lives, who has kept me from harming you, if you had not come quickly to meet me, not one male belonging to Nabal would have been left alive by daybreak' (1 Sam. 25:32–4)

If you must tell another person what someone did to you – because you can't contain the pain – then tell only one person, someone who won't repeat it. I only hope they will be as faithful to you as Josif was to me.

When we *should* speak of the grievance

What about the rapist? The child abuser? Should not the authorities know? What about church discipline? Can one totally forgive and report a malady or crime at the same time as totally forgiving? Yes – I will say more about this below, but I must say now that total forgiveness does *not* mean closing our eyes to those who will continue to harm others. The apostle Paul ordered that the incestuous man in Corinth be put out of the church lest the entire church become corrupted (1 Cor. 5:5). The rapist therefore should be apprehended. Child abusers should be reported to the police before they reoffend.

What I am mainly writing about in this book is not so much pertaining to a crime that has been committed, or the church bedevilled with scandalous sin. Rather, harbouring a grudge because you want revenge is what this book is about. Wanting to 'get even' is what has to be dealt with.

There is admittedly a very thin line between the desire to see the rapist or child abuser imprisoned and sticking to the principle that such a person is a danger to society. As we will see below, when we are personally agitated we usually disqualify ourselves from removing the speck from another's eye (Matt. 7:5). But a person who has been raped needs to be a witness in a courtroom while simultaneously forgiving the offender. In no way do I say this is easy. But let us first make some clarifying points as to what total forgiveness is not – and then what it is.

What total forgiveness *is not*

1 Approval of what they did

God never approved of our sin; he hates sin. Jesus forgave the adulterous woman, but he did not approve of what she did. He told her, 'Leave your life of sin' (John 8:11). God was angry with our first parents, Adam and Eve, but made garments of skin for them and clothed them (Gen. 3:21). This immediately showed that he had forgiven them. The garments of skin meant the sacrifice of blood that pointed towards the Redeemer who was to come. So God did not approve of what they did – or approve of our sin today. 'But with you there is forgiveness; therefore you are feared' (Ps. 130:4).

So too with us. Forgiving people does not mean approval of their evil. We forgive what we don't approve of because that is the way God is with each of us.

2 Excusing what they did

We do not cover up for them. We do not point to circumstances that explain away their behaviour. It is true that 'every person is worth understanding', as Dr Clyde Narramore says, but that does not excuse them.

Moses was offered a 'new deal'. God said to him – in so many words – 'You have a sorry lot of people to lead, and they aren't following you very well. They have been stubborn and unteachable. I am going to wipe them off the face of the earth and start all over again – with a new nation' (see Num. 14:11–12). But Moses rejected the offer; he interceded for them. However, he did not excuse their behaviour, but instead appealed to God's mercy: 'In accordance with your great love, forgive the sin of these people, just as you have

pardoned them from the time they left Egypt until now'
(Num. 14:19). And God forgave them.

3 Justifying what they did

To justify means to make right or just. The *Oxford Dictionary*
says it means 'to show (a person or statement or act, etc.) to be
right or just or reasonable'. There is no way that evil can be
justified; God never justified evil and does not require us to
do so.

In the above incident regarding Moses and the Israelites,
Moses did not offer a hint of justification for their behaviour.
Instead he pointed out to God that the Egyptians would not
think very highly of God's power or name if they were
obliterated. Therefore when we are required to forgive we are
not required to make what is wrong look right.

4 Pardoning what they did

A pardon is a legal transaction which releases an offender
from the consequences of an action, such as a penalty. This is
why we do not ask that the guilty rapist be exempt from
punishment. He needs to pay his debt to society and ensure
that society will not live in fear of him.

I knew of a lady who was raped by a person from a Middle
Eastern country. She did not know he was from overseas at
the time but found this out later after he was caught. In the
meantime she became a Christian. The police wanted her to
testify. She was told that this rapist could be sent back to his
country and that that might mean his execution. She turned
to me, and I advised her to testify against this man. She had
already forgiven him – and did not want to get him into
trouble for vindictive reasons. But had she not come forward,
he would likely have raped again. By the time she testified she

had no bitterness, but merely described what happened. The man was sent back to his own country; we will probably never know what happened to him after that.

5 Reconciliation

Forgiveness and reconciliation are not always the same. Reconciliation takes two people, and the person you forgive may not want to see you. They may even be dead. Moreover, you may not want to be the best friend of the person you forgive.

Reconciliation means a restoration of friendship after a quarrel. When a husband and wife totally forgive each other it will usually mean a reconciliation – but not always. The bitterness and the desire to punish may be gone, but the wish to have things as they were may not necessarily be so strong. If one's spouse is unfaithful and sleeps with one's best friend, that friendship will probably never be the same again, although the bitterness and desire for revenge need to go. An injured person can forgive an offender without reconciliation. It is wonderful indeed should reconciliation follow, but this must not be pressed in some cases. Some things can never be the same again. It takes two to reconcile, a total willingness on both parts.

God was in Christ, reconciling the world to himself (2 Cor. 5:19). But we still implore people on Christ's behalf: 'Be reconciled to God' (2 Cor. 5:20). Why? The reconciliation doesn't really exist unless both parties agree.

6 Denying what they did

By this I mean repressing what they did. Repression – suppressing what we feel – is almost always unconscious. Some people, for various reasons, live in 'denial' – that is, refusing to admit or come to terms with the reality of a bad situation. It is sometimes painful to face reality, and an easy way out (we wrongly think) is to deny that this has happened.

Repression is almost always a bad thing to do, but we often do it involuntarily because the pain seems too great to take on board. And yet we don't really get rid of the pain: we push it down into the 'cellar' of our subconsciousness, but it comes out in the 'loft' of our lives – as high blood pressure, anxiety, irritability or even a heart attack.

Much child abuse is repressed. One cannot believe that a parent, a trusted friend or relative would do such a thing, so one lives in denial – often blaming oneself. The victims of rape often do the same thing.

Total forgiveness is not achieved by repressing what has happened. It is only true and total forgiveness when we come to terms with reality – 'this person actually did or said this' – and then forgiving them.

7 Blindness to what happened

Some people, especially those with an 'overly scrupulous conscience' (as some Puritans may call it), feel that to forgive is to be wilfully and consciously blind to what someone has done. They feel that if they are blind to the offence they are actually forgiving the person, but if they *see* the offence they are keeping a record of wrongs. They feel it is better, then, to be blind to it – as if it never happened. But this is not total forgiveness either.

Wilful blindness is slightly different from repression. Blindness is a conscious choice to pretend; repression is usually unconscious and involuntary.

Both are wrong and can be psychologically damaging, because when we play games with ourselves like this, though the motive may be to forgive, we delay coming to terms with our responsibility. In some cases the same person who meant to forgive explodes one day – all because they were not being true to themselves – and everybody is shocked. It is not total forgiveness until you admit to *seeing* what they did – and *then* you set them free.

Paul said that love keeps no record of wrongs (1 Cor. 13:5), but he did not mean that you are blind to those wrongs. Some think that a way of forgiving is to pretend that no wrong is there. The Greek word *logizetai* means to 'reckon' or 'impute'. It means essentially that 'love does not store a wrong', – that is, the wrong doesn't go into our 'mental computer' to be reckoned with later on. We would say today: love doesn't allow a wrong to be computed. But that there *is* wrong staring you in the face is not to be denied. In fact, the Greek word translated 'wrong' is *kakon*: evil. The wrong – the evil – is acknowledged; we are not blind to it; we are not required to pretend it didn't happen. This is not what total forgiveness means.

Love is never blind to the hurt. If the person who hurt us is an authority figure or, let us say, known to be very 'godly', we say to ourselves, 'I didn't see this. I didn't hear this. This could not have happened; therefore it didn't.' The truth is, sometimes the people we admire most can be very mean and do hurtful things. It is of no value to pretend that we didn't see.

8 Forgetting

When someone says we must 'forgive and forget' I understand what they mean. But literally to forget may not be realistic; it might even be impossible. We may, owing to a deep trauma, temporarily forget things. But the only way back to sanity is to try to remember everything – in detail.

Love doesn't erase our memories. Furthermore, it is a demonstration of great grace when we are fully aware of what they did – and still choose to forgive totally. Deep hurts may not be eradicated as though they never happened. The truth is, they *did* happen. We cannot easily forget them. We certainly must not dwell on them but we cannot always forget them.

Even God doesn't literally forget our sins: he *chooses* to overlook them. He knows full well what we have done and what he has forgiven us of – every sordid detail. But he chooses not to remember, so that he doesn't hold them against us (Heb. 8:12). That is precisely what *we* are to do, choosing not to remember while maybe not forgetting.

9 Refusing to take the wrong seriously

We cannot truly forgive until we see the actual thing we are forgiving, and how serious it is.

Some may think they are to dismiss a wrong out of hand, or pass it off as inconsequential or insignificant. They may even think this is forgiving the offence, but that is only avoiding the problem – possibly trying to make forgiveness easier. The greater victory for the one who does the forgiving is to face up to the seriousness – possibly a high-handed wickedness – of what they did; and still to forgive.

This is what God does: there is no sin too great for God to forgive. But he equally knows exactly what it is we've done and what it is he is forgiving. He doesn't say, 'Come now, my dear, that's not too bad. I can easily wash *this* sin away.' No. He knows what we have done, which is why he sent his Son to die; he doesn't pass a sin off as inconsequential, but instead he forgives. Totally.

10 Pretending we are not hurt

It is ridiculous to think that we should have to keep that stiff upper lip – when we have been betrayed, molested, unjustly criticised, or injured by a spouse's infidelity.

God let David know how grieved he was over the king's adultery and murder: God did not pretend *not* to be hurt. David was a man after God's own heart (1 Sam. 13:14) and yet God was ruthlessly impartial with David. He was very grieved indeed.

Even Jesus was obviously hurt when he was struck in the face by a high priest's official. This is why he asked, 'Why did you strike me?' (John 18:23.) After all, Jesus endured the cross and scorned (not denied) the shame (Heb. 12:2).

What total forgiveness *is*

1 Being aware of what someone has done and still forgiving them

As we saw above, total forgiveness is not being oblivious to what someone has done, covering up for them, excusing them, or refusing to see exactly what was wrong. This is to live in denial, like some people do during a time of grief when a loved one dies. Sooner or later they must come to terms with reality. As I said, repression is almost never a good thing. In any case it is no spiritual victory to think we are forgiving people when we are only avoiding facing up to their wrong. It is, if anything, evading true forgiveness. It is as though we are saying to ourselves, 'I want to forgive them but I don't think I really could if they actually did what they appear to have done.' So we postpone recognising what they really did in order to keep us from experiencing the pain of letting them carry on as though nothing has happened.

Total forgiveness is only fulfilled when we know what someone has done without any denial or covering up for them – and yet still refusing to make or let them pay. It is a wonderful victory when we forgive in this manner, but it is no victory at all if we are not fully aware of the evil we choose to forgive.

Total forgiveness is painful. It hurts when we kiss revenge goodbye. It hurts to think of that person getting away with what they did and nobody knowing. But when I know fully what they did, and accept in my heart that they will be blessed without any consequences for their wrong, I have crossed over into the supernatural. This means I have begun to be a little bit like Jesus.

2 It is a choice to keep no records of wrong

Love 'keeps no record of wrongs' (1 Cor. 13:5). Why do we keep records? To use them. To prove what happened. To wave it before someone who doubts what actually happened.

A husband may say to his wife in a moment of anger, 'I'll remember that.' And he does! She may say to him, 'I can never forget this.' And she doesn't! So many marriages could be healed overnight if *both* parties would stop pointing the finger. Pointing the finger, a common problem in human history (Isa. 58:9), shows that one has kept a record of wrongs.

Love is a choice. Total forgiveness is a choice. It is not a feeling – at first – but an act of the will. It is the choice to tear up the record of wrong. As we observed above, we clearly see the evil that was done, but we erase it – or destroy the record – before it becomes lodged in the heart. This way, resentment does not have a chance to grow. But when we say, 'I'll remember that', when we have been hurt or maligned, we fertilise the soil then and there for an abiding resentment.

When we develop a lifestyle of total forgiveness we learn to erase the wrong rather than file it away in our mental computer. When we do this all the time – that's what I call a lifestyle – we not only avoid bitterness, but experience total forgiveness as a feeling. It is not initially a feeling; it is a painful choice at first. But *later* we feel it – and it is a good feeling.

3 Refusing to punish

This is the essence of total forgiveness. It is when we give up the natural desire to see them 'get what's coming to them'. By nature we cannot bear the thought that they have got away with what they have done; it seems so unfair. Therefore we want vengeance – namely, their just punishment. The fear that they won't get punished is the opposite of perfect love. This is why John said: 'There is no fear in love. But perfect love drives out fear, because fear has to do with punishment. The man who fears is not made perfect in love' (1 John 4:18).

When perfect love – the love of Jesus and the fruit of the Holy Spirit – enters, the desire for our enemy to be punished leaves. When the desire for one to be punished gains entrance, the anointing of the Spirit subsides.

Therefore total forgiveness is refusing to punish. It is refusing to cave into the fear that this person or those people won't get their 'come-uppance' – the punishment or rebuke we think they deserve.

I have long been intrigued by the phrase in the New International Version that fear 'has to do with punishment' (1 John 4:18). This means many things, but partly it means our fear that God won't step in and give 'them' their just deserts. But if one gives into this fear we will be trespassing on God's territory, and he doesn't like that. Vindication is God's prerogative and God's prerogative alone. Deuteronomy 32:35 – 'It is mine to avenge; I will repay' – is quoted twice in the New Testament (Rom. 12:19; Heb. 10:30). Vindication is what God does best. He doesn't want our help. So when we refuse to punish – and God likes that – it sets him free to decide what should be done. But if we manœuvre our way into his expertise he may well let us do it, but neither divine vengeance nor true justice will be carried out – only our personal grudge.

It is therefore important that we examine ourselves in this area. We must ask ourselves, how much in what I am about to say or do is but an attempt to punish? If it is, we grieve the Holy Spirit however much right may be on our side.

4 Not telling what they did

As I said above, there may be a need to tell somebody about your own hurt, and this can be therapeutic. But you should tell maybe only one other person and be sure that person will never repeat it.

Telling a person with the purpose of hurting another's reputation or credibility is but wanting to punish them. That is why we usually tell – not so much for therapeutic reasons but to keep our enemy from being admired. I tell what that person did to me so that you will think less of them. It is my attempt to punish – which is usurping God's arena of action.

But when I recall that total forgiveness is forgiving others as I have been forgiven it means: (1) I won't be punished for my sins; and (2) nobody will know about my sins, for sins under the blood of Christ will not be exposed or held against me. Therefore when I blurt out what 'they did to me' I am apparently forgetting that God will not tell what I did to him. He has forgiven me and won't tell. Therefore when I tell on my enemy I am not only showing contempt for my own

28

forgiveness but I am trying to punish them as well – which God doesn't like one bit.

I know that I have said that one may share with another person, for therapeutic reasons, the wrong that we have suffered, and I believe that my conversation with Josif Tson that day falls into this category. There is no doubt that it has 'worked together for good' (Rom. 8:28 AV). And yet the funny thing is, had I the light and knowledge I now have on this subject I would never have told Josif in the first place. You may want to say that some of us are better off for my story (I've told it all over the world) – which is also why this very book has come along – and I would have to agree. But I have learned from this, and have had not a few episodes since that I might be tempted to share with someone but I know I must not. If you do share your hurt with someone, I would urge you to be very sure that you aren't doing it to punish the 'offender' by making them look bad:

> Who steals my purse, steals trash;
> 'Twas mine, 'tis his, and has been slave to thousands.
> But he that filches from me my good name
> Robs me of that which not enriches him,
> And makes me poor indeed.
>
> From *Othello*, by William Shakespeare

5 Being merciful

'Blessed are the merciful, for they will be shown mercy' (Matt. 5:7). There is a sense in which the Bible basically says two things about God: (1) that he is merciful, and (2) that he is just. The heart of the gospel is related to these two characteristics of God. The greatest question we can ask when it comes to the gospel of Christ is: how can God be just and merciful at the same time? By merciful, it means that God does not want to punish us; by just, it means he must punish us because we have sinned against him. So how can he be both simultaneously? Answer: he sent his Son Jesus Christ – the God-man – who died on a cross for us. 'We all, like sheep, have gone astray, each of us has turned to his own way; and the LORD has laid on him the iniquity of us all' (Isa. 53:6). Because God punished Jesus for what we did, he can now be true to himself and still be truly merciful to us. That is the heart of the gospel.

But when we are told to be godly – which means being like God – it does not follow that we can be like him in every sense. After all, God is omnipotent (all-powerful) and we are not commanded to be that. He is omnipresent (present everywhere) and we can never be that. So too when it comes to carrying out punishment, *this belongs to God alone*, as we must continually emphasise, and never, never underestimate.

When it comes to being merciful, this is our Lord's command: 'Be merciful, just as your Father is merciful' (Luke 6:36). In the Greek language this is the opposite of wrath or justice. Being merciful is not giving justice, but the opposite. One difference between grace and mercy is that grace is getting what we *don't* deserve (favour) and mercy is not getting what we *do* deserve (justice). So when we show mercy we are withholding justice from those who have injured us. That is godliness.

There is a fringe benefit in this for us if we show mercy: we will be *shown mercy*. This goes to show that total forgiveness is not devoid of an element of self-interest: 'The merciful man doeth good to his own soul' (Prov. 11:17 AV).

6 Graciousness

This is showing grace and mercy at the same time. There is an interesting Greek word *erikes*, that means 'forbearance' or 'tolerance'. It comes from a root word that means the opposite of being unduly rigorous. In Hellenistic literature Aristotle contrasted it with severely judging. The idea was: do not make a rigorous stand even though you are clearly in the right.

In Philippians 4:5 it is translated 'gentleness' ('moderation' in the Authorised Version). It comes down to our English word 'graciousness'. It is an exceedingly rare quality. It is a word that cuts right across a legalistic spirit (which comes naturally to many of us). It is a concept that is quite threatening to those of us who don't suffer fools gladly, we who feel that being inflexible for the truth is the ultimate virtue. Paul used the word *erikes* in the context of a family squabble in Philippi between Euodia and Syntyche: 'I plead with Euodia and I plead with Syntyche to agree with each other in the Lord' (Phil. 4:2). If only each of them would be gracious. Both had strong personalities, each probably had a following; each side was so sure that they had got it right. Each wanted the other to look bad. 'Try graciousness,' says Paul. It is an unusual virtue.

It is a word that describes Jesus all the time. When a group of self-righteous religious leaders led a woman to Jesus who was found in the act of adultery, there was no question that sin had taken place. But what was our Lord's attitude? Graciousness. They wanted to see if he would throw the book at the woman. 'When they kept on questioning him, he straightened up and said to them, "If any one of you is without sin, let him be the first to throw a stone at her" ' (John 8:7). One by one, the accusers slipped away. 'Jesus straightened up and asked her, "Woman, where are they? Has no-one condemned you?" "No-one, sir," she said. "Then neither do I condemn you," Jesus declared. "Go now and leave your life of sin" ' (John 8:10–11). In this case it was not a question of *whether* wrong had taken place. But our Lord's attitude was to be gracious.

Graciousness is not the way presidential elections are won. In 1988 former US president George Bush's Campaign Manager claimed two facts: (1) candidates with high negative ratings in the opinion polls – above 35 per cent – lose; and (2) negative ratings are far easier to create than positive ones. In other words, to win it is not enough to look good; you must make your opponent look bad. It works.

But graciousness is withholding certain facts you know to be true. It is demonstrated by what you *don't* say, although what you could say would be true. Self-righteous people find it almost impossible to be gracious; they claim always to be after 'the truth'.

Total forgiveness is graciousness that will sometimes mean overlooking the truth, and not letting on that you know anything that could damage a person in any way.

7 It is an inner condition

Total forgiveness must take place in the heart for otherwise it is worthless. 'For out of the overflow of the heart the mouth speaks' (Matt. 12:34). If we have not truly forgiven, in our hearts, those who have hurt us, then it will come out – sooner or later. But if forgiveness has indeed taken place in the heart, our words will show it. When there is bitterness, it will eventually manifest; when there is love, 'there is nothing in him to make him stumble' (1 John 2:10), even in our words.

It is for this reason that reconciliation is not always essential to total forgiveness. If it takes place in the heart, one does not need to know whether one's enemy will reconcile. If I have forgiven him or her in my heart of hearts, and he doesn't want to speak to me, I can still have the inner victory. It is true that it is far easier to forgive when we know that those who maligned or betrayed us are sorry; but if I must have this before I can forgive, I may never ever have a victory.

If someone tells me that I am not required to forgive unless the other person repents first and says, 'I'm sorry', then I answer: Jesus' example on the cross is good enough for me. 'Jesus said, "Father, forgive them, for they do not know what they are doing." And they divided up his clothes by casting lots' (Luke 23:34). If he had waited until they felt any guilt or shame for their words and actions, then Jesus would never have forgiven them.

It is my own experience that most people we must forgive do not believe they have done anything wrong whatsoever; or if they did something wrong they believe it was justifiable. I would go so far as to say that 90 per cent (at least) of all the people I've ever had to forgive would be indignant at the thought that they had done something wrong. If you put them under a lie-detector test they could honestly say that they have done nothing wrong whatsoever – and they would pass the test with flying colours.

Total forgiveness therefore must take place in the heart; and if it is a genuine experience in the heart, I will not be devastated if there is no reconciliation. For if those who hurt me don't want to make up, that isn't my problem when I have totally forgiven them. This is also why a person can achieve victory within even in the case of forgiving the person who has died. 'Dear friends, if our *hearts* [my italics] do not condemn us, we have confidence before God' (1 John 3:21). Confidence towards God is ultimately what total forgiveness is all about; it is he I want to please at the end of the day. He cares and knows whether I have truly and totally forgiven, and when I *know* I have his love and approval I am one very happy and contented servant of Christ.

8 It is the absence of bitterness

Bitterness is an inward condition. It is an excessive desire for vengeance that comes from deep resentment. It heads the list of the things that grieve the Spirit of God (Eph. 4:30ff.). It became Esau's preoccupation (Gen. 27:41) and is one of the most frequent causes for people to miss out on the grace of God: 'See to it that no-one misses the grace of God and that no bitter root grows up to cause trouble and defile many' (Heb. 12:15). The bitterness will manifest itself in many ways – losing your temper, high blood pressure, irritability, sleeplessness, an obsession with getting even, depression, isolation, a constant negative perspective, and feeling unwell generally.

Inside therefore we must begin to get rid of a bitter and unforgiving spirit for otherwise the attempt to forgive will fail. It is true that doing the right thing even if you don't feel like it can lead on to one having the right feeling. But the very act of doing right, or trying to, shows that the bitterness is not as deep as it could be. In other words, even when we feel bitter but begin to put the principle of total forgiveness into action (see Chapter 2), it shows that we are not totally controlled by bitterness – for otherwise we wouldn't make a start in doing what is right.

The absence of bitterness allows for the Holy Spirit to be himself in us. This means that I will be very like Jesus. When the Spirit is grieved I am left to myself, which means I will struggle with emotions ranging from anger to fear; but when the Holy Spirit is ungrieved, he is *at home* in me – he will be all that he wants to be in me. I will be able to think clearly and manifest the gentleness of the Spirit, but bitterness in me chases the Dove away. A high level of bitterness is a virtual guarantee for having no peace of mind, but getting rid of it is an open invitation for the Holy Spirit to give you his peace, joy and knowledge of his will.

This is extremely important when it comes to the matter of reconciliation. Let us say, for example, your best friend has had an affair with your wife. Must you forgive him? Yes, but it does not follow that you will remain close friends. If I have totally forgiven the person who has hurt me – that is, I have no bitterness – then I need not feel the slightest guilt or shame for not wanting a complete restoration of that relationship. Or even if there never was a friendship in the first place, but someone wants to destroy me, I must totally forgive them – and see it as entirely reasonable that I don't want to lunch with them every Sunday.

The essential factor then is that there should be no trace of bitterness. But how can I know that there is no bitterness left? I would reply: (1) when there is no desire to get even or punish, (2) when I do or say nothing that would hurt their reputation or future, and (3) when I truly wish them well in all they seek to do.

9 Forgiving God

Although we often do not see it at first – and for some it takes a long time – all our bitterness is traceable to our anger towards God. It may be an unconscious anger – some good people would be horrified at the thought that they have bitterness towards God. But we repress this too; such knowledge is too painful to admit to. The truth is, our bitterness is often aimed at God.

Why? Because he allowed bad things to happen. Since he

is all-powerful and all-knowing, he could have prevented these things from happening. He has allowed us to suffer when we didn't do anything that we know of to warrant such ill-treatment. Therefore what we are ultimately thinking is that God is to blame for our hurt.

Only a fool would claim to know the full answer to the question 'Why does God allow evil and suffering to continue when he has the power to stop it?' But there is a partial answer: namely, in order that we may believe. There would be no need for faith if we knew the answer concerning the origin of evil and the reason for suffering. I only know it is what makes faith possible. But I know something else: 'And we know that all things work together for good to them that love God, to them who are the called according to his purpose' (Rom. 8:28 AV). God does turn evil into good. He causes things to work together for good. God did not send his Son into the world to explain evil, but rather to save us and to exemplify suffering. Jesus who was, and is, the God-man suffered as no one else has. One day God will clear his name from the charge of being unjust. In the meantime, we need to trust him and take him at his word that he is just and merciful.

As for all the unhappy things he has allowed to happen to me, I affirm his justice. He is God. He knows exactly what he is doing and why; he knows why he allows things to take place that he could have stopped.

For those who struggle with God's right to allow evil – and we have all done this – there still must be a genuine forgiveness on our part, for any bitterness grieves the Spirit. We therefore must forgive him – but not because he is guilty, but for allowing evil to touch our lives. But if we will lower our voices and patiently wait for God's purposes to be fulfilled, then one day – and this is a guarantee – we will say that he has done all things well, even in what he permitted. He was never guilty in the first place, but because he sometimes appears to us to have been unfair, we must set him free before we can effectively move on in our lives.

10 Forgiving ourselves

Total forgiveness, then, means forgiving people – totally – and also forgiving God. But it also means forgiving ourselves – totally.

It is a common complaint that any church leader hears: 'I know God forgives me, but I can't forgive myself.' This is so important that we will come back to it later. But I must say here and now: there is no lasting joy in forgiveness if it doesn't include forgiving myself. It is anything *but* total forgiveness if we forgive God and those who have hurt us, but are unable to forgive ourselves. It is as wrong as not forgiving others, because God loves us as much as he does others and will be as unhappy when we don't forgive ourselves as when we hold a grudge against others. In a word: we matter to God. He wants our joy. He not only wants us to forgive ourselves but wants it urgently.

Total forgiveness brings such joy and satisfaction that one is tempted to call it a selfish enterprise. As we have seen, the wider research that is taking place these days has already overwhelmingly concluded that the first person to experience delight when forgiveness takes place is the one who forgives.

I pray that what has been written and what follows will challenge you and motivate you, more than ever, to forgive those who have hurt you, to forgive the God who let it happen, and to forgive yourself – totally.

2

How do we know that we have totally forgiven someone?

Then Joseph could no longer control himself before all his attendants, and he cried out, 'Make everyone leave my presence!' So there was no-one with Joseph when he made himself known to his brothers. And he wept so loudly that the Egyptians heard him, and Pharaoh's household heard about it. Joseph said to his brothers, 'I am Joseph! Is my father still living?' But his brothers were not able to answer him, because they were terrified at his presence. Then Joseph said to his brothers, 'Come close to me.' When they had done so, he said, 'I am your brother Joseph, the one you sold into Egypt! And now, do not be distressed and do not be angry with yourselves for selling me here, because it was to save lives that God sent me ahead of you. For two years now there has been famine in the land, and for the next five years there will not be ploughing and reaping. But God sent me ahead of you to preserve for you a remnant on earth and to save your lives by a great deliverance. So then, it was not you who sent me here, but God. He made me father to Pharaoh, lord of his entire household and ruler of all Egypt. Now hurry back to my father and say to him, "This is what your son Joseph says: God has made me lord of all Egypt. Come down to me; don't delay. You shall live in the region of Goshen and be near me – you, your children and grandchildren, your flocks and herds, and all you have. I will provide for you there, because five years of famine are still to come. Otherwise you and your household and all who belong to you will become destitute." You can see for yourselves, and so can my brother Benjamin, that it is really I who am speaking to you. Tell my father about all the honour accorded me in Egypt and about everything you have seen. And bring my father down here quickly.' Then he threw his arms around his brother Benjamin and wept, and Benjamin embraced him, weeping. And he kissed all his brothers and wept over them. Afterward his brothers talked with him. (Genesis 45:1–15)

After my life was changed by taking Josif Tson's advice on board, I began to preach the message of total forgiveness in a variety of places. But people began coming up to me with this question: 'How do I know I have totally forgiven?' They would sometimes say, 'I think I have, but I'm not sure I really have.'

The truth is, I didn't know how to answer them. I even began to wonder whether *I* had really totally forgiven those people who had hurt *me* so much. I began to search for a way to find out.

I found it – unexpectedly. I began preaching on the life of Joseph (Gen. 37–50) in June 1982. I remember the date well because this series of sermons began on the first Sunday night in June, immediately after Arthur Blessitt had preached for me on five Sunday nights in a row in May 1982. This is the man who has carried the cross around the world, who holds the record in the *Guinness Book of Records* for the world's longest walk. I invited him to preach for us at Westminster Chapel. He turned us upside-down! This is when we began to sing worship songs (instead of only the traditional hymns), when we began our Pilot Light ministry (witnessing on the streets between Victoria and Buckingham Palace on Saturday mornings), and when we started inviting people forward to confess Christ publicly after the Sunday evening services. On the first Sunday night in 1982 I gave my first appeal for people to come forward after the service: seven came. That was also my first sermon on the life of Joseph. Those sermons also make up my book called *God Meant it for Good*.

In Genesis 45 we have the account of Joseph revealing his identity to his brothers. It is in these verses that we find a heart-searching frame of reference by which we can know whether we have totally forgiven people. Until I came across this chapter in that series I was uncertain when I tried to explain whether we had truly and totally forgiven people. But here we have a very clear indication because that is exactly what Joseph had to do, and did: totally forgive his brothers.

Joseph and total forgiveness

The background is this. Twenty-two years earlier, Joseph's brothers had conspired to kill him, because they were jealous of him. He was his father Jacob's favourite child. Jacob had made a richly ornamented robe ('coat of many colours', AV) which Joseph, the arrogant seventeen-year-old teenager, strutted around in. On top of that, Joseph told his brothers dreams he had had that indicated that the eleven brothers would one day come begging to him. Joseph showed no sensitivity or humility at all:

> He said to them, 'Listen to this dream I had: We were binding sheaves of corn out in the field when suddenly my sheaf rose and stood upright, while your sheaves gathered round mine and bowed down to it.' His brothers said to him, 'Do you intend to reign over us? Will you actually rule us?' And they hated him all the more because of his dream and what he had said. Then he had another dream, and he told it to his brothers. 'Listen,' he said, 'I had another dream, and this time the sun and moon and eleven stars were bowing down to me.' (Genesis 37:6–9)

It doesn't take Sigmund Freud to interpret those dreams! And yet, the dreams were from God. There was nothing wrong with Joseph's gift – which had to do with dreams – but there was a lot wrong with Joseph. God's hand was in fact on Joseph but this young man needed a lot of sorting out. God allowed Joseph's brothers to deal with him ruthlessly. However, instead of killing him they decided on Plan B – selling him as a slave to the Ishmaelites. This they did, never expecting to see him again.

In the meantime, the brothers concocted a clever cover-up. They dipped that richly ornamented robe in goat's blood and then took it to their father Jacob. Deceitfully they said this to him, 'We found this. Examine it to see whether it is your son's robe' (Gen. 37:32). The plan worked:

He recognised it and said, 'It is my son's robe! Some ferocious animal has devoured him. Joseph has surely been torn to pieces.' Then Jacob tore his clothes, put on sackcloth and mourned for his son many days. All his sons and daughters came to comfort him, but he refused to be comforted. 'No,' he said, 'in mourning will I go down to the grave to my son.' So his father wept for him. (Genesis 37:33–5)

But God was with Joseph. He began work in the house of an Egyptian officer whose name was Potiphar – to whom the Ishmaelites had sold Joseph. Joseph was so appreciated there that he was put in charge of the entire household. But some time later Potiphar's wife began to flirt with Joseph, who is described as well-built and handsome. 'Come to bed with me!' she pleaded; Joseph refused. 'Hell hath no fury like that of a woman scorned,' said Victor Hugo. After repeatedly rejecting her, she decided to accuse Joseph of rape. The next thing we know is that Potiphar has Joseph put in prison. In other words, for doing the right thing Joseph was punished! But Peter said, 'For it is commendable if a man bears up under the pain of unjust suffering because he is conscious of God. But how is it to your credit if you receive a beating for doing wrong and endure it? But if you suffer for doing good and you endure it, this is commendable before God' (1 Pet. 2:19–20).

This was the beginning of an era of preparation for Joseph – not that he knew this. However, God had great plans for Joseph. Dr Lloyd-Jones used to say to me, 'The worst thing that can happen to a man is to succeed before he is ready.' God wanted to ensure that Joseph did not come out of prison or embark on the next phase of his life's work until he was ready. 'Because the Lord disciplines those he loves, and he punishes everyone he accepts as a son' (Heb. 12:6).

Joseph had much to be bitter about. First, what his brothers had done to him. True, he made them jealous and he was not a very nice guy – he was even a tattle-tale (Gen. 37:2). But plotting to kill him, or selling him to the Ishmaelites, never expecting to see him again, was a wicked and evil act. Secondly, Joseph was falsely accused. Instead of sleeping with Potiphar's wife, he resisted the temptation. We all like to think that God will bless us when we are faithful and obedient to his word, but the thanks Joseph got was imprisonment. Thirdly, God allowed it all. Joseph's rationale for resisting Potiphar's wife's overtures was loyalty to God – how could I do this and 'sin against God?' he explained to her (Gen. 39:9). A lot of people I know are afraid to have an affair for but one reason: the fear of getting caught. Here Joseph was in Egypt where nobody knew him (and his family back in Canaan would never know) and Potiphar's wife certainly wasn't going to tell! But Joseph was faithful because he didn't want to displease God – and now God lets Joseph go to prison for something he didn't do.

A lot to be bitter about, then, and many to forgive: his brothers, Potiphar's wife who lied, and God who let it all happen.

Joseph got company in prison after a while – Pharaoh's cupbearer and baker. Each of them had a dream. Joseph offered to interpret them – and got them right. Sadly, he predicted that the baker would be hanged in three days (which happened), but that the cupbearer would get his job back in three days (which he did). So far, so good.

But a temptation too great – so it seemed – was handed to Joseph on a silver platter. Before he could barely finish telling the cupbearer he would be restored to Pharaoh's favour, Joseph got too involved in his prophetic word: 'But when all goes well with you, remember me and show me kindness; mention me to Pharaoh and get me out of this prison. For I was forcibly carried off from the land of the Hebrews, and even here I have done nothing to deserve being put in a dungeon' (Gen. 40:14–15).

Most of us would have said the same thing, but God had such special plans for Joseph that there should be no promotion but that which could be explained in terms of what God alone could do. In other words, God wanted Joseph out of prison as much as Joseph wanted out. If the cupbearer simply put in a good word for Joseph and he got released from prison, then that would have been relief – but far short of what God had in mind from the beginning. This goes to show that delays can be part of God's purpose; seemingly unanswered prayer can be as much a part of God's will as answered prayer.

The truth is, Joseph needed to be delivered from bitterness and self-pity, and this had not happened yet. How do we know? First, 1 Corinthians 13:5, the same verse that says love 'keeps no record of wrongs', says that love 'is not self-seeking'. This means that we will not play 'man the manipulator' when it comes to promoting ourselves; we must let God do it. Joseph was, secondly, still full of self-pity. He says so: 'I have done nothing to deserve being put in a dungeon' (Gen. 40:15). Self-pity and self-righteousness – twin sins – are eclipsed when we are prepared to forgive totally and keep no record of wrongs. In a word, Joseph – at that point in time – had not yet forgiven his brothers, Potiphar's wife, or God.

Joseph would not have forgotten his dreams. He knew that one day – for some reason or other – his brothers would come begging to him.

They did – but when it happened Joseph was a changed man. No bitterness. No grudges. None. Something had happened to him during those next two years. How do we know? Well, look at him, listen to him! He has totally and wonderfully forgiven them all, whereas he probably used to fantasise about that day when they would come begging, longing for the day he could look at the fulfilment of those old dreams and say to them, 'Gotcha!', and then throw the book at them. But no. He lovingly welcomed them and forgave them with tears.

What happened was this. Two years later Pharaoh himself had a dream – two dreams in fact. Nobody could interpret them – not even his magicians and astrologers, who were paid for this sort of thing could figure them out. The cupbearer overheard the commotion and remembered and recommended Joseph. Suddenly Joseph was brought before Pharaoh. He interpreted the dreams: there will be seven years of plenty of food followed by seven years of famine. Joseph said that Pharaoh should save food during the first seven years so that there would be food during the second seven years – not only for Egypt, but also for the surrounding countries who would have to come to Egypt begging for food.

Pharaoh was so impressed that he made Joseph the Prime Minister of Egypt right on the spot! Yet God did it all. He used the cupbearer, yes – but not because of Joseph's manipulation. The cupbearer would have remembered Joseph anyway.

During the famine, who do you suppose came begging for food? Yes, Joseph's brothers. He recognised them instantly, but they didn't know who he was – he was twenty-two years older and in official Egyptian garb, not to mention speaking Egyptian through an interpreter. So the moment came when Joseph revealed himself to his brothers. It was the moment he dreamed of: the day of the fulfilment of those dreams.

But instead of throwing the book at them (which he had the power to do), he wept. Filled with love, he demonstrated total forgiveness.

Applying Joseph's example to ourselves

So how does the example of Joseph help us?

1 Do not let anybody know what someone said about you or did to you

This is exactly what Joseph was ensuring when he cried out, 'Make everyone leave my presence!' (Gen. 45:1.) So there was no one with Joseph. My guess is that all left except the interpreter, because until then Joseph had never communicated with his brothers directly but only through an interpreter (Gen. 42:23). The interpreter had no idea that Joseph could speak Hebrew with his brothers, but then, to his surprise, he too was told to leave. It is clear that there was no one with Joseph when he decided to make himself known to his brothers.

But why? Why make everybody leave? Because Joseph did not want a single person in Egypt to know what his brothers had done to him twenty-two years before. He had a plan: namely, to persuade them to bring their father, Jacob, to Egypt. He wanted his entire family there with him, but he did not want anybody in Egypt to know what they had done to him.

Joseph was the hero of Egypt: the people were in awe of him. By interpreting Pharaoh's dreams he had saved the nation, but he knew that if word leaked out that his brothers had actually kidnapped him and sold him to the Ishmaelites, the people would hate his brothers. But Joseph wanted his brothers to be heroes in Egypt – just as he was. This was the only way to ensure that nobody in Egypt would ever discover their wickedness. He allowed no one present to eavesdrop this historic conversation when he was revealing his identity to those startled, frightened men. And not only did Joseph not let anybody know what they had done: he ensured that they *could* not know. That is one of the proofs that one has totally forgiven.

And that is precisely how you and I are forgiven. 'As far as the east is from the west, so far has he removed our transgressions from us' (Ps. 103:12). Our sins are 'wiped out' (Acts 3:19). It is as though our sins don't exist any more – they are gone, gone, gone, gone! As far as our eternal standing and security with God are concerned, they will never be held against us. Back in the hills of Kentucky we used to sing a chorus that says our sins are buried in the 'sea of God's forgetfulness'. This is based on Micah 7:19: 'You will again have compassion on us; you will tread our sins underfoot and hurl all our iniquities into the depths of the sea.'

This means that God will not reveal what he knows. Picture if you will a large, giant screen like we have at Westminster Chapel for projecting worship songs. Imagine your sins listed on that screen for people to see. You would look at those sins described and have to admit, 'Yes – that's true. But I thought I was forgiven and that nobody would know.' Imagine the sense of betrayal you would feel if God disclosed what he knows about you!

By the way, there's a lot God knows about me that I wouldn't want you to know about. He has enough on me to bury me. But you will never know. God won't tell.

But why do we tell? If merely for therapeutic reasons, then to tell one other person who will never repeat it is understandable. But, as we have seen, the real reason we usually tell is to punish. *We want them punished.* And one weapon at our disposal is the tongue. We tell what we know to make others look bad! If we can hurt their credibility or reputation for hurting us, we say, 'Good, it serves them right.' So we blab to people about what someone did as a way of getting even with them.

Joseph is sometimes depicted as a 'type of Christ'. That generally refers to someone in the Old Testament who makes you think of Jesus before Jesus himself came along. And despite his imperfections, Joseph was indeed a 'type' of Christ in many ways. His ability to forgive his brothers as he did is what Jesus did with his disciples. Almost scared to death and feeling so ashamed over the way they had deserted Jesus when he was arrested, the disciples were behind closed doors when the resurrected Jesus turned up unexpectedly and just said, 'Peace be with you!' (John 20:21.) Those disciples were totally forgiven – and they knew it.

We all have skeletons in the cupboard; some known, some unknown. It is comforting to know that God freely and totally forgives and will never tell what he knows. That is the way Joseph forgave. That is why we are urged: 'Be kind and compassionate to one another, forgiving each other, just as in Christ God forgave you' (Eph. 4:32).

2 Do not allow anybody to be afraid of you or intimidated by you

Joseph revealed his identity to his brothers with tears and compassion for them. The last thing he wanted was for them to be afraid of him. He had been aching for days to let them know who he was, but had to follow a carefully thought-out strategy before he could be sure the plan would work. But when he could 'no longer control himself' he broke down and wept as he told them who he was.'And he wept so loudly that the Egyptians heard him, and Pharaoh's household heard about it' (Gen. 45:2).

Joseph's immediate concern was not only to reveal who he was, but also to know how his father was: 'Joseph said to his brothers, "I am Joseph! Is my father still living?" But his brothers were not able to answer him, because they were terrified at his presence' (Gen. 45:3).

When we have not totally forgiven those who have hurt us, it gives us a bit of pleasure to sense that they are afraid or intimidated. If, when we walk into a room with several people and see one who has hurt us (and knows it) and they freeze with anxiety, we say to ourselves, 'Good!', then it shows there is still bitterness in our hearts. For perfect love casts out fear, which has to do with punishment (1 John 4:18). Therefore if people are afraid, we fancy they are getting a bit of punishment – which is what we want.

But not Joseph. Knowing they were 'terrified at his presence' he said to them: 'Come close to me.' Why? For two reasons: (1) he did not want them to be afraid, and (2) he was longing to embrace every single one of them – which he later did.

Fear can cause us to do silly things. It is because of our insecurity that we want people to stand in awe of us. Therefore we are pretentious; we try to keep them from knowing who we really are and what we are really like. Sometimes I think the most attractive thing about Jesus as a man was his unpretentiousness. Jesus did not try to create an aura of 'mystique'; he was the type of person that ordinary people could relate to.

And here was Joseph, ascending as high as one could get in

terms of prestige and power. He might have kept those brothers at a distance; he might have wanted them to praise him for excelling as he had obviously done. Here was a chance for them to fall at his feet in fear and reverence. He might have said, 'Remember my dreams?' He might have reminded them of their disbelief when he told them that this day would come. 'I told you so,' he might have said.

No. 'Come close to me,' he said. He did not feel a cut above them. There was no desire for them to stand back and say, 'Wow! This is our brother Joseph.' And he wanted no fear on their part. He wanted to be loved rather than admired.

Paul said, 'For you did not receive a spirit that makes you a slave again to fear, but you received the Spirit of sonship. And by him we cry, "*Abba,* Father" ' (Rom. 8:15). The word *Abba* is a pure Aramaic word that is the equivalent of 'Daddy'. The witness of the Holy Spirit makes us feel loved and accepted, and God does not want us to be afraid of him once he has forgiven us. Not that this means we develop a cheap familiarity with him, much less lose a sense of his glory and might; and yet we feel his fatherly tenderness.

What Joseph wanted his brothers to feel is what Jesus wants us to feel – about him and the Father. 'Anyone who has seen me has seen the Father,' said Jesus (John 14:9). You may understandably have trouble relating to God as Father because of having had an abusive or absentee father yourself. But whoever said we had to have perfect fathers before we could rightly relate to our heavenly Father? The perfect image is Jesus: what Joseph was trying to convey to his brothers. There was not a trace of fear or need in Joseph for these men to show further remorse; Joseph wanted them to love him and feel his love for them.

This is what Jesus seeks to do with all of us; he wants to

put us at ease in his presence. When Jesus met with the Eleven in the upper room after his resurrection, there was no hint of saying, 'How could you do this? Why? How could you have deserted me like that?' No. He just picked up where he left off before the whole ordeal began and said, 'As the Father has sent me, I am sending you' (John 20:21). There is no fear in love (1 John 4:18). Joseph did not want his brothers to be afraid. When we have totally forgiven, we will not want people to be afraid.

3 We will want them to forgive themselves and not feel guilty

When the eleven brothers finally edged a little closer to Joseph, he repeated, 'I am your brother Joseph, the one you sold into Egypt!' (Gen. 45:4.) This shows that he had neither forgotten nor pretended that they hadn't done what they had done; he was simply identifying himself to them.

Knowing exactly their fears and what they were thinking, he said: 'And now, do not be distressed and do not be angry with yourselves for selling me here' (Gen. 45:5). He was not about to send them on a 'guilt trip'; he knew already that they felt guilty enough (Gen. 42:21).

Sometimes we may say to someone, 'I forgive you for what you did, but I hope you feel bad about it.' This shows we still want them punished. It shows our own fear which, I will repeat, 'has to do with punishment' (1 John 4:18). When fear is gone, the desire to have them punished goes with it.

One way we love to punish is to make people feel guilty. For those of us who are always sending people on a 'guilt trip', it is almost certainly we ourselves who have the biggest problem of all with a sense of guilt. Because we haven't sorted out our own guilt, we want to make sure that others wallow in the mire of guilt with us. We point the finger partly because we haven't forgiven ourselves.

I sometimes think guilt is the most painful feeling in the world. I can't say this for sure, because I haven't suffered the extent of emotional or physical pain that some have. But I know none the less that my own greatest pain over the years is guilt – and to be reminded of my own failure (especially as a parent). If someone wanted to hurt me – really and truly make me feel awful – all they have to do is to ask, 'How much time did you spend with your kids in those critical years as they were growing up?' But you will be pleased to know that I believe my children have totally forgiven me.

Joseph wanted to set his brothers free. He did not want them to blame themselves or be angry with themselves; he wanted them to forgive themselves. As we have seen and will see further below, forgiveness is worthless (in so far as the emotional benefits go) if we can't forgive ourselves. And it certainly isn't *total* forgiveness unless we forgive ourselves as well as others.

God knows this, and this is why he wants us to forgive ourselves as well as to accept his promise that our past is under the blood of Christ. And Joseph was trying to do what Jesus would one day do: make it easy for his brothers to forgive themselves.

Then Joseph added: 'Because it was to save lives that God sent me ahead of you' (Gen. 45:5). God does that with us; he wants to make it easy for us to forgive ourselves. That is partly why he gave us what is possibly Paul's most astonishing promise: 'And we know that all things work together for good to them that love God, to them who are the called according to his purpose' (Rom. 8:28 AV). God doesn't want us to feel guilty, so in effect he says to us: 'Just wait and see, I will cause everything to work together for good to such an extent that you will be tempted to say that what happened was good and right.' Not that it *seemed* good — for the fact that all things work together for good, it must be repeated, doesn't necessarily mean that it felt right at the time. But God has a way of making events *come* good.

This is total forgiveness: not wanting people to feel guilty or upset with themselves for what they have done, and showing them that there is a reason why God let it happen.

4 We will let them save face

This is carrying the previous principle of total forgiveness a step further, for Joseph now said what is without doubt the most magnanimous, gracious and emancipating thing he had said so far — *you* didn't do it, *God* did: 'But God sent me ahead of you to preserve for you a remnant on earth and to save your lives by a great deliverance. So then, it was not you who sent me here, but God. He made me father to Pharaoh, lord of his entire household and ruler of all Egypt' (Gen. 45:7–8). This is as good as it gets. When we can forgive like that, we're there. Saving face; this is what God does with each of us.

What is 'saving face'? Dale Carnegie uses this expression in his book *How to Win Friends and Influence People* (1937). Although this is not a specifically Christian book, it would do most Christians I know no harm to read it, for it is saturated with Christian principles. Saving face means preserving your dignity and self-esteem. It is not only the refusal to let a person feel guilty; it is providing a rationale that enables what they did to look good rather than bad. Or it may mean hiding a person's error from people so they can't be embarrassed.

You can make a friend for life by letting that person save face. I gather this is an oriental expression, because for an oriental the worst thing on earth is to lose face. Some have been known to commit suicide rather than lose face. But I have a suspicion we are all the same when it comes to saving or losing face. God lets us save face by causing our past (however foolish) to work together for good. If you read Matthew 1:6, part of Jesus' genealogy, you would have thought that Bathsheba's and David's sin was all along part of the divine strategy. I doubt it. David's sin of adultery – and the attempted cover-up by murdering Uriah – must rank with the worst crimes of Israeli history. But not according to Matthew 1:6; God lets us believe that what happened was as if it was supposed to be.

Can you imagine the look on the faces of those men when Joseph said to them, 'So then, it was not you who sent me here, but God' (Gen. 45:8)? Reuben may have said to Judah, 'Did we hear correctly? That we didn't do what we did but rather God did it?' To have believed a word like that would have meant an unimaginable burden of guilt rolling off these men. For those who bore the shame of such folly, to hear that God was actually behind it was news too good to be true.

But how could this be, Joseph? The answer is simple: God predestined that Abraham's descendants would live in Egypt. He simply 'sent me ahead of you'. In other words, Joseph was virtually saying, 'Somebody had to go first and I was chosen.' God knew about the famine and that the family of Israel needed to be preserved.

There is more, though. By saying what he did Joseph was also admitting that he would have done what they did had he been one of them. He did not condemn them for what they did; he too would have reacted to such arrogance in the same way had he been them.

The one who totally forgives from the heart has little self-righteousness, for one of the reasons we are *able* to forgive is that we see what we ourselves (1) have been forgiven of, and/ or (2) are capable of. When we are indignant over someone's wickedness there is the real possibility that either we are self-righteous or that we have no objectivity about ourselves. When we see ourselves as we are we will see that we may well be capable of any sin ever committed by anyone save by God's intervening grace.

This was no self-righteous man reaching out to his brothers; Joseph was not condescending to them, or patronising them, or conscious that he was achieving any great feat. He was not thinking, 'I will be admired for being so gracious to these unworthy, evil men.' In fact, quite the contrary. Joseph had forgiven these men during those two years in the dungeon when God worked on his heart. That is the only explanation for the profound change in Joseph. In a word: he was a trophy of sovereign grace, but was blind to any heroism in his making himself known to his brothers.

Letting them save face, then, was not a polite gesture; Joseph was telling his brothers the truth. God *had* meant it for good; God *did* send Joseph on ahead. He was not one whit better than a single one of them, and he was not about to act as if he were a cut above them. He wasn't, and he knew it. He just felt grateful to see them, but he was also grateful to God that he had been chosen to go to Egypt first. After all, look at the wonderful things that had happened to him as a result! The preparation, the false accusation, their conspiracy, and the cupbearer not remembering him at first, were worth it all. It is like when Jesus said to his disciples: 'A woman giving birth to a child has pain because her time has come; but when her baby is born she forgets the anguish because of her joy that a child is born into the world. So with you: Now is your time of grief, but I will see you again and you will rejoice, and no-one will take away your joy' (John 16:21–2). The pain Joseph went through to get to where he was now was all forgotten.

When we let people save face we are doing what is right and just, not being merely magnanimous and gracious.

5 We will protect them from their greatest fear

What do you suppose these eleven men were now thinking? They were no doubt thrilled to their fingertips that their brother had really and truly accepted them. The relief must have been sweet beyond words to describe, but no sooner than they could absorb this would come the greatest fear of all: that they would have to return to Canaan only to tell their father the truth of what they had done.

You can be sure that they'd rather have died than have to face their aged father with the truth of what actually had happened when they laid that bloodstained coat of many colours before him. Their worst nightmare was that their father would find this out. And now they were faced with the prospect of returning to Canaan and then persuading their father to come and live in Egypt where his beloved Joseph was – would you believe – the Prime Minister.

Joseph knew their fears. He had already calculated this; he was a step ahead of them, knowing their guilt and dread of such a nightmare. He knew that his forgiving them of what they had done twenty-two years earlier was utterly worthless to them if they had to tell the whole truth to their father.

This to me is one of the most moving parts of this scenario. Joseph instructed his brothers to tell their father that Joseph was alive and well and had become Prime Minister of Egypt. Indeed, he told them exactly what to say to him. What is striking is what they were *not* to say. It was worded so carefully that they were not allowed to reveal all that had happened. Notice carefully the language of Genesis 45:9–13. It is a speech that Joseph had prepared for them to recite to their father. In a word: Joseph would not allow them to tell their father the whole truth. And why should they? Would Jacob be better off by knowing it? No. Would they be better off telling Jacob? No. Would Joseph be better off? No.

Sin that is under the blood of our Sovereign Redeemer does not have to be confessed to anybody but to God. If you need to tell it to one other person because of what it will possibly do for you, fine. But you do not need to involve an innocent party by unloading information on them that they can easily live without. More often than not, those who confess their sinful past – including infidelity – are sorry that they told anybody. For example, that wife or husband is not better off knowing of a spouse's former unfaithfulness now that it is over. Leave it behind. Confess it to God. 'Against you, you only, have I sinned and done what is evil in your sight, so that you are proved right when you speak and justified when you judge' (Ps. 51:4).

You may say that these men should have confessed their sin to their father, Jacob. Really? And given Jacob an even greater problem – having to struggle with the lost years and with bitterness against his sons?

Joseph was wise, loving and fair. It made his brothers all the more respectful of him.

When I consider that our Lord Jesus Christ knows all about us but promises to keep what he has forgiven a carefully guarded secret, it makes me all the more indebted and thankful to him. Not that Joseph was doing it for that reason; he only wanted to set his brothers free and give them a wonderful future. But it no doubt endeared them to him all the more.

The same brothers (other than Benjamin) had been so nervous and scared up until then. But Joseph convinced and won them over, for it says, 'Afterward his brothers talked with him' (Gen. 45:15).

Many of us have one single greatest fear of a certain thing being revealed. I know I do. I know what I would fear the most – were it to be told. But God has no desire for this; the only possibility of that occurring would be if I became self-righteous and unforgiving. (We will deal below with Matthew 6:14–15 in this respect.) In the meantime, I am indebted to a wonderful Saviour who forgives all and will ensure that my greatest secrets will not become known.

God does not blackmail us, and if a Christian is guilty of this, it gets God's attention. He won't stand for it. To hold another person in perpetual fear because I constantly threaten, 'I'll tell' – when I know what I myself have been forgiven of – would bring down God's wrath on me more quickly than anything. When I ponder for very long what I have been forgiven of, it is enough to shut my mouth for the rest of my life.

6 It is a life-long commitment

This means that you keep on doing it – as long as you live. It won't do to forgive today and then return to folly tomorrow. I knew of a person whose wife said, 'I thought you forgave me.' He replied, 'That was yesterday.' Total forgiveness is a life-long commitment; you may need to do it every single day of your life until you die. No one said it would be easy.

Seventeen years later Jacob died, and Joseph's brothers suddenly panicked. They reckoned that Joseph's forgiveness lasted only so long as the aged patriarch was still alive, but when he died they feared that Joseph would at long last get his vengeance. One can understand their fears, for what Joseph did was no ordinary thing. They had been blessed by his graciousness, but they feared it had come to an end. 'When Joseph's brothers saw that their father was dead, they said, "What if Joseph holds a grudge against us and pays us back for all the wrongs we did to him?" ' (Gen. 50:15.)

In my opinion, the brothers concocted a story: 'So they sent word to Joseph, saying, "Your father left these instructions before he died: 'This is what you are to say to Joseph: I ask you to forgive your brothers the sins and the wrongs they committed in treating you so badly.' Now please forgive the sins of the servants of the God of your father" ' (Gen. 50:16–17). Had Jacob really said this, he would have told Joseph himself. He would not have gone to the grave with a fear like that. It was the brothers who feared.

But when Joseph heard this message, he wept. He felt disbelief. He could see that they lived in fear that one day he, the Prime Minister, would use his power to get vengeance on his brothers: 'But Joseph said to them, "Don't be afraid. Am I in the place of God? You intended to harm me, but God intended it for good to accomplish what is now being done, the saving of many lives. So then, don't be afraid. I will provide for you and your children." And he reassured them and spoke kindly to them' (Gen. 50:19–21).

This shows that what Joseph had done seventeen years before still held good. It shows how deeply he meant it then and that he was prepared to care for them indefinitely. 'I forgave you then and I forgive you now,' he was saying to them. This does indeed show that Joseph's change of heart was no passing thing. It was real. And yet, genuine though the change was, he *might* have had second thoughts later. I have known some people who have caved in after they have done so well in achieving forgiveness. But it is not *total* forgiveness unless it lasts – no matter how great the temptation to turn back. I wonder if this partly explains Psalm 85:8: 'I will listen to what God the LORD will say; he promises peace to his people, his saints – but let them not return to folly.'

I know that in my own case the temptation to be bitter was very real. There were times when I would have conversations in my head, imagining what I might say, or recalling what took place, and it was then that I would get churned up. The thought that 'nobody will ever know' or 'they are getting away with this' would agitate me. But as soon as I lost peace, I could see the folly of such thinking. I had to keep on forgiving. Total forgiveness goes on and on and on, and some days will be harder than others.

This means that I must never tell what I know, allow my 'offender' to feel fear, want them to feel guilty, hope they will lose face, or reveal that thing that I know that would devastate them most of all. And I must keep this up for as long as I live.

Therefore if you are prepared to make a covenant to forgive – and to forgive totally – you must realise that you will have to renew it again tomorrow, otherwise it isn't total forgiveness. It may even be harder to do it tomorrow than it is today. It could even be harder next week – or next year. This is a total life commitment.

7 Praying for them to be blessed

In addition to the aforementioned six principles, I would have to add another, although I can't show this from the life of Joseph. He may have done this (I wouldn't be surprised if he did), but I can't prove it. We touched on it in the previous chapter: you pray for those who have wronged you: 'But I tell you: Love your enemies and pray for those who persecute you' (Matt. 5:44). When you do this as Jesus intends it, you are being set free indeed. Yet carrying this out is a life's work.

To pray for the one who has hurt you means to pray that they will be blessed. That God will bless them and show favour to them rather than punish them. You pray that they will prosper. In a word: you pray that they will be dealt with as you want God to deal with you. You apply the Golden Rule as you pray (Matt. 7:12). You don't pray, 'God, deal with them.' You don't pray, 'Get them for what they did.' And neither is it enough to say, 'Father, I commend them to you.' That's a cop-out. You pray that they will be totally forgiven just as you want to be yourself.

And yet praying like this, to quote John Calvin, 'is exceedingly difficult'. Chrysostom (*c.* 344–407) called it the very highest summit of self-control. And yet Job's suffering did not begin to turn around until he prayed for those 'friends' who had become his thorn in the flesh (Job 42:10). But when we do this we are becoming like our heavenly Father (Matt. 5:44ff.). That is true godliness, the quintessence of Christ-likeness.

To me the greatest motivation to live like this is Stephen. He is one of my heroes. When I think of the Spirit on him – his enemies being unable to withstand his wisdom, the miracles he did, and his radiant countenance (Acts 6:8–15) – I say to myself: 'I'd give anything in the world for that kind of anointing.' His secret, however, emerged at the end of his life. When they were stoning him he prayed – seconds before his death – 'Lord, do not hold this sin against them' (Acts 7:60). There lies the secret to his unusual anointing.

If therefore you ask, 'How can I know I have totally forgiven my enemy, my betrayer, my unfaithful spouse, my unkind parent, the one who ruined my life or the one who has hurt my children,' I would answer: carrying out these seven principles is, I think, as near as you can get to exhibiting *total forgiveness*.'

I must add one caution: never go to a person you have had to forgive and say to them, 'I forgive you.' This will be counterproductive every time unless it is to a person that you happen to know is yearning for you to forgive them. Otherwise, you will create a stir that you will not be able to cope with. They will say to you, 'For what?' It is my experience that nine out of ten people I have had to forgive sincerely do not feel they have done anything wrong. It is up to me to forgive them from my *heart* – and then keep quiet about it.

3

The Lord's Prayer and forgiveness

This is how you should pray:

'Our Father in heaven,
hallowed be your name,
your kingdom come,
your will be done
on earth as it is in heaven.
Give us today our daily bread.
Forgive us our debts,
as we also have forgiven our debtors.
And lead us not into temptation,
but deliver us from the evil one'

For if you forgive men when they sin against you, your heavenly Father will also forgive you. But if you do not forgive men their sins, your Father will not forgive your sins. (Matthew 6:9–15)

It may seem surprising to some that people who are not Christians can learn to forgive; yet we saw this implied in the Introduction. We also saw that there are *degrees* of forgiveness. It would be my view that a person who is not a Christian could demonstrate what may be called limited forgiveness and feel all the better for it. If a person is sufficiently motivated, one may achieve a great deal of inner satisfaction by overcoming bitterness. Mahatma Gandhi appealed to one's sense of valour and heroism when he said, 'The weak can never forgive. Forgiveness is the attribute of the strong.' On the other hand, President John F. Kennedy said, 'Forgive your enemies, but never forget their names.' That is hardly *total* forgiveness!

The Bible urges us to forgive – totally. For this reason it is very surprising indeed to learn that there is no teaching of this kind of forgiveness in Judaism. After the Holocaust there was a consensus that the Jewish people would never forget – ever. Therefore the idea of a Jew becoming a believer in Jesus as Messiah and then praying with a Palestinian believer is unthinkable for the majority of Jews today. But that is happening – even in Israel as you read these lines. One wishes that this sort of thing would happen in Britain where often people try to justify their bitterness – even Christians!

Forgive us our debts

I suppose that the fifth petition of the Lord's Prayer, 'Forgive us our debts, as we also have forgiven our debtors' – or 'Forgive us our trespasses as we forgive those who trespass against us' – has made liars out of more people than any document in human history. But don't blame Jesus for that. We should mean what we say if we choose to pray the Lord's Prayer. And Jesus did not say we had a choice; he said, 'This is how you should pray.'

I want to show what Jesus regarded as the most important petition in this prayer and what we are saying when we pray, 'Forgive us our debts.' It is obviously a plea for forgiveness, but then comes the assurance – or possibly the big lie: 'As we also have forgiven our debtors.' This petition is both a plea for forgiveness and a claim that we have already forgiven those who have hurt us. In an equivalent section, Luke 11:4, Jesus says, 'Forgive us our sins, for we also forgive everyone who sins against us.' There it is in the present tense, claiming that we are forgiving everyone. Perhaps it is a promise that you will do it, but in the version of the Sermon on the Mount in Matthew 6:12, it is promising God that we have *already done it*: 'Forgive us our debts, as we also have forgiven our debtors.'

I have prayed that this chapter will make a difference in the lives of those who read it. That means I have prayed for you. I have a suspicion that there are many who do need this teaching – and some who need it desperately. I don't want you to have false guilt; I don't want to make anybody feel condemned. I don't want anyone to feel threatened by these lines. But if you can take this word and apply it, I believe that this chapter can make a difference in your life. By the way, do you often pray the Lord's Prayer? You should. It is the most complete and perfect prayer ever designed.

Do you realise what you are saying when you pray this petition, 'Forgive us our debts, as we also have forgiven our debtors'? You are praying to God that you will be forgiven all your sins. Now the word translated 'debt' comes from a Greek word which simply means 'what is owed'. It is used inter-changeably with 'sins'. Right after the prayer is finished, Jesus goes on to say, 'If you forgive men when they sin against you.' That shows that he meant 'sin' when he said 'debt', and if there is any further doubt, in Luke's version he uses the word 'sin'. It means 'what is owed to God', and because you owe him pure obedience, coming short of it means you are indebted to him and that you ask him to wipe off that debt.

So when you pray, '*Forgive* us our debts' or '*Forgive* us our trespasses', you are asking God to let you off the hook. 'Forgive' comes from a Greek word which means 'to let be' or 'to send away'. For example, 'to let be' would mean that God will not do anything to you; he just lets you stay as you are and just wipes away what you owe. Or 'to send away' means that your sins will be sent away and you are not liable for them. So instead of having to pay, God just lets it go. We thus ask God to wipe our debts away.

This, however, is not a prayer for becoming a Christian; it is not a prayer to be saved, nor is it what we call the 'Sinner's Prayer'. The 'Sinner's Prayer' is summed up in the words, 'God be merciful to me, a sinner.' That is essentially the way a person comes to Christ (Luke 18:13). For if we pleaded for salvation on the basis that we had already forgiven others, then it would be a conditional salvation. We would be reckoning that we cannot be saved unless we can point to our having forgiven everybody – as if God then would say, 'OK, now I will save you.' But then we could only *keep saved* as long as we *keep forgiving* everybody, and if we stopped we would lose our salvation. So if the Lord's Prayer were a prayer for the non-Christian to pray, it would be a prayer for a conditional salvation – based on good works.

It is a prayer that only a believer – one who can truly, with Jesus, call God 'Father' – can pray.

The truth is that Jesus himself acknowledges what the Bible

generally affirms. 'Who can say, "I have kept my heart pure; I am clean and without sin"?' (Prov. 20:9.) 'There is not a righteous man on earth who does what is right and never sins' (Eccles. 7:20). 'There is no-one who does not sin,' said Solomon as he prayed for the dedication of the Temple (1 Kings 8:46). 'If we claim to be without sin, we deceive ourselves and the truth is not in us' (1 John 1:8).

What is the purpose of the Lord's Prayer?

What, then, is the purpose of this prayer? Not to appeal to our own strength, but to keep us in fellowship with the Father. 'But if we walk in the light, as he is in the light, we have fellowship with one another, and the blood of Jesus, his Son, purifies us from all sin' (1 John 1:7). In order to have fellowship with the Father, because God is light and in him there is no darkness at all (1 John 1:5), all of our sin must be cleansed, and that is true if we are walking in the light. Walking in the light partly means taking with both hands *anything God shows you.* But if he shows you something and you sweep it under the carpet, years later you will wonder why you haven't grown over the years; you have postponed obedience, there is no real fellowship with the Father.

The Lord's Prayer is also designed to keep us from feeling self-righteous. Now we all have this problem, and we have to fight it every day. We naturally want to justify ourselves; we instinctively want to point the finger. This prayer will help to keep us on our toes spiritually and helps to give us objectivity about ourselves. That means seeing ourselves as we really are. This prayer therefore shows that we need daily forgiveness as much as we need daily bread.

There are two things that Jesus takes for granted in the

Lord's Prayer. The first is the assumption that people have hurt us. The second assumption Jesus takes for granted is that we will need to be forgiven. We all have come short of *God's* glory and Jesus wants us to realise that he knows that people also come short of treating *us* with the dignity, love and respect that we would like. Jesus therefore assumes that we have been hurt by others. We have hurt God and we want to be let off the hook; people have hurt us so we must let them off the hook.

In what way have you been hurt by people? Perhaps you have been discredited, or dishonoured; you have been disappointed that they could be so ungrateful. You have been lied about; been taken advantage of; people haven't been very appreciative; they have been disloyal. So think of somebody around you who has discredited you. Think of somebody around you who has disappointed you because they are not grateful. You want another person to show their thanks. If they say 'Thank you', you say, 'Don't mention it', but if they hadn't said it, you would have noticed! You do want to be thanked, you do want them to feel grateful, and when it is obvious that they are not grateful, it gets to you. Jesus is telling us that that is the way people are.

You may not realise it, but you too do that to somebody. Would you like them to let *you* off the hook? You therefore pray that God won't throw the book at you and you pray that God won't throw the book at them.

I remember one critical time in my life when I wanted to get closer to God and I also knew that I had to forgive. It was as though God stopped me in mid-sentence and said, 'R.T., do you know what you are asking? This means you are wanting me to forgive them and to bless them.' For it is one thing to say to God, 'Forgive them', but be hoping he doesn't.

It is another thing to say it and mean it. In that moment, I had to decide. Did I want God to take me seriously, truly to forgive them and let them off the hook?

Do you want God to let *you* off the hook? As I said above, we've all got skeletons in the cupboard. What if God decided, because you won't forgive, that he's going to pull a skeleton out of your cupboard and let everybody know what he knows about you? That is a pretty good motivation, if you ask me, to say, 'God, forgive them, yes, thank you very much, forgive them.'

Forgiveness is a life-long commitment

Not only do we need daily forgiveness as we need daily bread, but we also need to pray daily to forgive others because doing this, as we have seen, is a life-long commitment. It is not easy; no one said it would be easy. I will say once again, this is the hardest thing I have ever had to do, but the Lord's Prayer is the way forward to fellowship with God. There is no forgiveness for the one who does not forgive; but it is not a prayer for justification, neither is it a prayer for keeping yourself saved. It is a prayer for continued fellowship. It means no pointing of the finger, no keeping a record of wrongs.

For as soon as Jesus finished with the Lord's Prayer, he adds: 'For if you forgive men when they sin against you, your heavenly Father will also forgive you' (Matt. 6:14). It is as though Jesus adds a P.S. to the Lord's Prayer. Having just finished the Lord's Prayer he says, 'For *if* [my italics] you forgive men when they sin against you, your heavenly Father will also forgive you' (Matt. 6:14). It is almost as though that is why he gave us the prayer in the first place!

Why does Jesus add this? Obviously it shows which of the

petitions was the most important. But there are other reasons too, for we can never get enough of this kind of teaching. I know I need to be reminded of this all the time. The most natural tendency in the world is to want to get your own back. It is as natural as eating or sleeping; you instinctively want to get even. But what Jesus is telling us to do here is something that is not natural, but supernatural – totally forgiving people (sometimes those closest to us) for what they have done to us. I have to tell you I still struggle here, and have to keep reminding myself. But when I truly and totally forgive, I have crossed over into the supernatural. One may not have experienced much of signs and wonders and miracles, or experienced many of the gifts of the Holy Spirit. But if we have totally forgiven those who have unjustly hurt us, in that moment we have crossed over into the supernatural realm – an accomplishment equal to any miracle.

The kingdom of heaven is the realm of the Holy Spirit. When the Holy Spirit is at home in us, it means he is ungrieved, he is himself; *he* doesn't adjust to *us*, but *we* have adjusted to *him*. We know the anointing of and intimacy with the Father. That is partly the meaning of the phrase 'kingdom of heaven'. It must be stressed again that when Jesus says, 'If you forgive men when they sin against you, your heavenly Father will also forgive you', he is not talking about the way to be saved. For if that *were* the way to be saved, then how many do you know who are *actually* saved if that is the way you become and stay a Christian? Jesus is not talking about how to be saved; he is talking about the anointing and intimacy with God. Neither is it a sinless perfection. After all, when he said, 'Forgive us our trespasses', he was assuming that we would all sin.

Being honest with ourselves about bitterness

Here's an even harder part, and I wish it weren't so. John says, 'If we claim to have fellowship with him yet walk in the darkness, we lie and do not live by the truth' (1 John 1:6). What is the darkness? The darkness is bitterness, as well as that confusion of mind and oppression in our hearts because we haven't really forgiven others. You may say, 'Oh, but I *am* having fellowship with God.' No. You just *claim* you are having fellowship with God if there is bitterness. If we claim to have fellowship with God but walk in darkness, then we lie. Walking in darkness is the consequence of not forgiving. When I don't forgive, I may still spend many hours a day in prayer, but I am not having genuine fellowship with God. If I can't forgive that person who has hurt somebody near to me, or if I can't forgive that person for whatever they did, then I am in darkness. I can preach and people may even say, 'Oh what a wonderful sermon; you must be having intimacy with God!' I can come and sing with my hands in the air and you may say, 'Oh look how R.T. is worshipping the Lord!' I could possibly put on such an act that you might think that I am the holiest person ever. In reality, if I have bitterness inside or am holding a grudge, I am just *claiming* to have fellowship with God, for really I am in darkness.

Jesus tenderly comes alongside in the Lord's Prayer and lets us know that we will be hurt by people we never dreamed would hurt us. We may think, 'Well, yes, I can imagine so-and-so hurting me, but I never thought it would be you!' 'Even my close friend, whom I trusted, he who shared my bread, has lifted up his heel against me' (Ps. 41:9). So this is a candid prediction from Jesus: we are going to be hurt by people. And that's not all: he calls this hurt that they do to us *sin*.

When people don't mean to hurt us

Now there is more than one kind of hurt. For example, sometimes people don't intend to hurt us, but we still get hurt. Sometimes they don't know they have hurt us. In other cases, though, they know they are disappointing us but don't want to: they don't have any choice. On occasions we have to take a decision that we know is going to upset someone, but we don't intend to hurt them; our motive is not to hurt. In fact, we would do anything we could to anaesthetise them, to ease the pain. As a parent or church leader one sometimes has to make decisions and say, 'I am sorry, but this is the way it's going to have to be!' Someone will be hurt and perhaps has to struggle to forgive. Over the years, I have also experienced it the other way round: where people have taken decisions concerning me. They knew that a certain thing would hurt me and it did – and I struggled. Their motive was not to upset me, but they still had to take this decision and I had to forgive them. So in cases like this it is not a sin you are having to forgive – but you are still hurt.

Hurt caused by insensitivity

There are those who are deliberately unkind – and that clearly is sin. There is also sin that is not wilfully committed, but none the less the person lacks sensitivity. A person can be so utterly insensitive that they deeply hurt another person. It may be that they are full of themselves; it could be that they are jealous. They may make decisions and say, 'Oh, there is no animosity here', but they are not aware that it is jealousy causing them to make that particular decision. It could be their own anger; their own ambition. Never forget we all sin every day, and we therefore should pray daily for those we have hurt unwittingly. Perhaps we have hurt them because we are not sensitive enough. The more sensitive I am to the Holy Spirit, the more sensitive I will be around a person in pain. That means I will not knowingly overlook a hurting person. Never forget the words about Jesus, 'A bruised reed he will not break' (Matt. 12:20). I always want to be that to every single person, but I fear that I am not. So the point is, there is one kind of sin where people are not malicious, they are not hateful, they are not wanting to hurt – but it is still sin because they are being insensitive.

Hurt caused by sins knowingly committed

And of course there are sins that are wilfully committed. People do wicked things, eyes wide open, and they know it. You say, 'Do I have to forgive that?' Yes.

But there is a wonderful consolation: the greater the sin you forgive them of, the greater the measure of the Spirit that will come to you. So if you have an extremely difficult case on your hands and you say, 'I can't forgive this!' you may not realise at first that there is being handed to you on a silver platter an opportunity to receive a measure of anointing that another person might never get because they don't have to forgive as deeply as you have to forgive! So if you have a deep hurt and you say 'I can't forgive!', then I want you to know there is great blessing that can be poured out on you which another person cannot achieve because they don't have the struggle that you have. Consider it a challenge, an opportunity; grasp it with both hands. Welcome the opportunity to forgive the deepest hurt, the greatest injustice; remember that a greater anointing is on offer.

What sins must we forgive?

What sin is it that we must forgive? Any sin. As we will see in more detail below, we must begin by not judging. That's not easy, but it is not for us to judge another's motives. Not judging is already the beginnings of forgiveness. We must leave it to God to judge how guilty they are. Whether what they did was deliberate or not, we only know that we are hurt. It may be they are like they are because of bad parenting. I am sure that all our children sooner of later will realise where we as parents have failed and will need to forgive us. I have had to forgive my father for his imperfections. Perhaps you have to forgive that unfair school teacher, your incompetent boss who has been promoted to a level beyond his or her competence. Moreover, you must forgive a fellow Christian who is insensitive.

Jesus is talking about a chosen privilege. 'If you forgive men' – that is, 'people' – that means you *choose* to do it, or you can choose not to. 'A man's wisdom gives him patience; it is to his glory to overlook an offence' (Prov. 19:11). Can you think of many things that can bring glory? Having a funeral at Westminster Abbey? Being given a knighthood? Winning a gold medal in the Olympics? Winning the Nobel Peace Prize? That's glory, but Proverbs 19:11 says, 'It is to a man's glory to overlook an offence.' That is doing something far more spectacular than winning an Olympic medal or being made a member of the House of Lords. It is glory *to overlook an offence*. It is crossing over into the supernatural.

Total forgiveness is a chosen privilege

Totally forgiving is a chosen privilege. It is a privilege to be godly: to be like God and pass this forgiveness on to someone else. Now, as I have already emphasised, it doesn't mean that this is the way to be saved. This is where people who don't believe 'once saved, always saved' are in difficulty. They say, 'Well, this verse shows that you can lose your salvation.' Wrong. I want to say to such people, no one would ever be saved if they had to maintain total forgiveness in order to get to heaven. Total forgiveness is something you grow into. It is achievable, it can be done, but it is not the way you are saved. It is the way you experience the Dove coming down and remaining on you (John 1:32ff.).

Why should you want to forgive? Because you prize fellowship with the Father more than your enemy being punished; You desire fellowship with God more than wanting God to throw the book at them. You want the anointing too much to get even with them.

But now Jesus puts it the other way around, just in case we didn't get the point already: 'But if you do not forgive men their sins, your Father will not forgive your sins' (Matt. 6:15).

This, then, is the continuation of our Lord's P. S. after the Lord's Prayer. We are hemmed in; there is no way we can avoid it. It shows that forgiving people is a 'no-joke matter'; it is serious, not an optional extra. And yet in order to motivate us to forgive, Jesus says, 'If you do not forgive, your Father will not forgive.'

What happens when we don't forgive?

What, then, is the result if we do not forgive?

If it means that we lose our salvation, then it follows that we are saved by works. I have to tell you, and make no mistake about it, that when you forgive another person that is a work – and a good work. But I would also remind you, 'For it is by grace you have been saved, through faith – and this not from yourselves, it is the gift of God – not by works, so that no-one can boast' (Eph. 2:8–9). But Paul adds, 'For we are God's workmanship, created in Christ Jesus to do good works, which God prepared in advance for us to do' (Eph. 2:10). So we are required to do good works, and one of those good works is forgiving those who have hurt us.

Although we know we are saved by grace alone, we still need to know what follows from our not forgiving. I therefore want to summarise some clarifications. It is vital for our theological understanding, as where there is confusion in this the turmoil and anxiety is endless.

1 Salvation is unconditional; fellowship with the Father is conditional

When we are justified before God we are declared righteous, and that comes by faith. For anyone who transfers the trust that he or she had in their good works and instead trusts what Jesus did on the cross, God credits to them a perfect righteousness. That is ours *for ever*. But fellowship with the Father *on our way* to heaven is conditional, because we may temporarily lose fellowship with the Father.

2 Justification before God is unconditional; the anointing of the Spirit is conditional

The anointing – the power of the Spirit in our lives – may ebb and flow. The Dove may come down and then flutter away for a while, but our standing before God, because of the righteousness of Christ put to our credit (Rom. 4:4–5), is permanent.

3 Our status in the family is unconditional; our intimacy with Christ is conditional

We are sons and daughters for ever; we have been adopted into the family (Eph. 1:5). We are as secure in the family as Jesus himself is in the Trinity. Why? We are made joint-heirs with Christ (Rom. 8:17). Once saved, always saved – but our intimacy with Christ is conditional.

4 Our eternal destiny – whether we go to heaven or hell – is fixed, but receiving a reward is conditional

Once we are saved we will go to heaven, but receiving an inheritance, which is a word that is often used interchangeably with reward (Col. 3:5), is conditional. Some may go to heaven without a reward: 'If what he has built survives, he will receive his reward. If it is burned up, he will suffer loss; he himself will be saved, but only as one escaping through the flames' (1 Cor. 3:14–15).

Thank God that all this is true, or there would be few, if any, ever saved! Yet having said that, totally forgiving another is an achievable thing. *It can be done*, and yet it is something you and I have to keep doing. It's not enough to say, 'Well, I did it yesterday, I have paid my dues, I showed I could do it'; it is instead a life-long commitment. Let no one say, 'That's beyond me!' It may be a continual struggle, but we can continually overcome and the consequences are wonderful. The opposite is just too awful.

God condemns an unforgiving spirit

God condemns an unforgiving spirit. 'If you do not forgive men their sins, your Father will not forgive your sins.' Why do you suppose God hates an unforgiving spirit? There are three reasons:

1 It shows an indifference to the greatest thing God did

This 'greatest thing' was God sending his Son to die on a cross for our sins. To be forgiven is the most wonderful thing in the world. In order to forgive us, God paid a severe price. I predict that when we get to heaven we will be able to see, little by little, what it meant for God to send his Son to die on a cross. We now only see the tip of the iceberg: we see waves of glory and these overcome us, but we've seen little. God did for us what we did not deserve. He therefore wants us to pass this on to others who don't deserve it.

2 We interrupt God's purpose in the world: reconciliation

How do we do this? God loves reconciliation and wants this to continue. He has given us the ministry of reconciliation, and when we are forgiven he wants us to pass it on. When we interrupt that, he doesn't like it at all. We therefore interrupt what he began: first, by sending his Son to die on a cross, effectually calling us by his grace and giving us total forgiveness. But we interrupt that flow by not passing it on.

3 God hates ingratitude

God loves gratitude. He knows what he has forgiven us of; he is fully aware of it. Read the account in Matthew 18 where the servant fell on his knees and went to his master and said, 'Be patient and I will pay you back everything', and the servant's master took pity on him and cancelled the debt and let him go. The master knew what he had forgiven the servant of. But then that particular servant went out and found one of his own servants who owed him one hundred denarii; he grabbed him and began to choke him and said, 'Pay back what you owe!' Then that servant did exactly what his master had done: fell on his knees and said, 'Please forgive me, I will pay you back.' The one who had been forgiven refused and threw his servant into prison. Word got back to the one who originally forgave, who of course knew exactly what he had forgiven that person of. To think there could be such ingratitude and anger!

Jesus then added, 'This is how my heavenly Father will treat each of you unless you forgive your brother from your heart' (Matt. 18:35). God knows what we have done. He knows what he has forgiven you of. There are things you have done, possibly that no one else will ever know about. You say, 'Well, they will never know', but God knows. If you turn right around and say, 'I can't forgive a person for this', he doesn't like it at all. He hates ingratitude. It shows we aren't very excited about having our sins forgiven; we are not very grateful. Therefore God judges us when we don't pass this forgiveness on. (How God does this will be seen in Chapter 4.)

How unforgiveness manifests itself

The characteristics of an unforgiving spirit usually begin with resentment; resentment is holding a grudge. It is when you are inwardly bitter, and preoccupied with hate and self-pity. You just can't come to terms with the possibility that this person, or those people, who did this to you will not be caught. You want them exposed; you want them to be held up for the whole world to see what they have done to you. The thought that this might not happen eats you up and the resentment goes so deep that you refuse to let them off the hook.

Resentment leads to going over and over in your mind 'what they did'. Re-counting. It's re-living exactly what happened. When it comes to those who have injured you, you should not do that – or even think about it. Instead of giving you relief and release, you will get even more churned up.

All this leads to wanting to get even. Revenge. You are determined to make them pay – not unlike the one who had been forgiven but who still said, in effect, 'Pay me back, pay me back!' (Matt. 18:30–32). He had been forgiven, but he couldn't pass that forgiveness on to another.

How then do you make them pay? One way is to say, 'I'll tell what I know about you', and then keep them paralysed with fear. Perhaps you know something about another, and if you spilled the beans about them it could ruin them. You would like to dangle it over them every so often and say, 'I still might tell.' Would Jesus do that? Do you have any idea how much it upsets God if you or I are like that?

There will be pay-day for those who won't forgive: 'But if you do not forgive men their sins, your Father will not forgive your sins' (Matt. 6:15). God intensely dislikes you or me holding another person as a hostage, and in fear, knowing what he has done in our case. We may do it by hurting their reputation. We may do it by keeping another from thinking well of that person. We may take this punishing further; we may want to administer the justice, really want to carry it out. Never mind that God says, 'Vengeance is mine!' Never mind that God says, 'This is something that only I do.' If *we* do it, it will be only a fraction of what God *would* have done. If you and I can't wait on God's timing and his manner and say, 'I'm going to make sure justice is carried out', then God says, 'You're on your own.'

Forgiveness is a choice we must make and it doesn't come easily. If it had been so easy, then why do you think Jesus mentioned it again after he finished the Lord's Prayer? He knows this isn't easy. It wasn't easy for God to do what he did, but God did it. He sacrificed his Son, and he asks us to make a little sacrifice by letting someone off the hook, and even *praying* that God will let them off the hook. When you do that and really mean it, *you are there*. God looks down from heaven and says, 'Good.' But you have to do it again tomorrow. You make the choice and you live with this. Love is an act of the will.

The choice *not* to let them remain unpunished, then, shows that we aren't sufficiently grateful that God has forgiven us. We haven't taken seriously how much we have sinned or that we are off the hook. Yes, what we all may want to do is to say, 'Well, what I have done isn't nearly as bad as what they have done!' And that's where we are wrong! This is being self-righteous. God hates self-righteousness as much as the injustice that you think is so horrible, and God certainly doesn't like it when we judge. So if you don't realise what God has forgiven you of, remember that the most heinous sin of all is self-righteousness.

I never will forget the time that this hit me. Some years ago I saw for the first time John Newton's hymn:

> In evil long I took delight
> Unawed by shame or fear;
> Till a new object struck my sight,
> And stopped my wild career.
>
> John Newton (1725–1807)

When I read those words I suddenly realised that I had had a wild career of being self-righteous, taking myself too seriously; I felt so ashamed.

If only we truly realised how much God hates self-righteousness – yet he will actually forgive us of that too! It could be argued that self-righteousness is the sin he hates most, and the hardest one for him to forgive. But he does it. You may say, 'I haven't had a sexual thought about that person' or 'I haven't fallen into immorality like this person'. Sexual sins *are* a serious business, but to God, self-righteousness is worse – for its very nature precludes awareness of sin.

A chief cause of an unforgiving spirit is self-righteousness. We choose not to let someone off the hook because we are not sufficiently grateful that God has forgiven us. For if we were, we would forgive.

Not valuing our fellowship with the Father

There is, however, another cause for an unforgiving spirit: namely, that we don't put a high enough value on fellowship with the Father. There is nothing more wonderful than fellowship with the Father; John said, 'And our fellowship is with the Father and with his Son, Jesus Christ' (1 John 1:3). Do you put a high value on fellowship with the Father? Moreover, does receiving a reward in heaven mean little or nothing to you? An unforgiving spirit means that you do not put a high value on things that one day will mean everything to you.

The consequences of an unforgiving spirit

What, then, are the consequences of an unforgiving spirit? What exactly does it mean when Jesus said, 'But if you do not forgive men their sins, your Father will not forgive your sins' (Matt. 6:15)?

1 The Holy Spirit is grieved

'And do not grieve the Holy Spirit of God, with whom you were sealed for the day of redemption' (Eph. 4:30). When the Holy Spirit is grieved it means a distortion in one's thinking. I urge you not to grieve the Holy Spirit because your relationship with him is the best thing you have got going for you. The ungrieved Spirit is what enables us to cope. I myself couldn't do my job if the Holy Spirit were permanently grieved. I cannot function or think clearly. If I have spoken a sharp word to my wife Louise, my children or someone around me, or if I have a bad attitude and feel resentment, trying to prepare a sermon is impossible. Why? Because resentment grieves the Spirit. It should be no different for you. You surely want to be at your best whether it is with computers, being a teacher, a postman, a lawyer, a salesperson, a nurse or a typist. You want to be at your best. You therefore do not want the Holy Spirit to be upset. We can never be reminded too often that immediately after Paul admonished us not to grieve the Spirit, he added:

> Get rid of all bitterness, rage and anger, brawling and slander, along with every form of malice. Be kind and compassionate to one another, forgiving each other, just as in Christ God forgave you. (Ephesians 4:31–2)

2 You are left to yourself

A refusal to forgive means that God slips away and lets you cope in your own strength. Not many people like that kind of life – coping in your own strength. I couldn't bear it. The Bible says the backslider is 'filled with his own ways' (Prov. 14:4 AV), so when one is left to oneself and to the flesh, those unthinkable capabilities towards sin in us are given leave to explode. Not only that; Satan gets in. He will take advantage of us if he can (2 Cor. 2:11). He will exploit that unforgiving spirit and ride on top of it. And you could at times even manifest a demonic spirit – all because this bitterness has so preoccupied you. *Not forgiving is an invitation to the devil to get in.* Satan will exploit your self-pity and the worst thing of all is that you may fancy that God is with you in this! It's like when the devil said to Eve, 'You will not surely die' (Gen. 3:4), and she said, in effect, 'Oh well, thank you for that!' and believed it. In your case, the devil will come in and say, 'Now look, normally it would be true that you should forgive, but what *you* have to forgive is so much worse than anybody else's grievance that God exempts you.' And you say, 'Oh, thank you for that!' – and are silly enough to believe it.

First, then, the Holy Spirit is grieved; you are not thinking clearly. Second, the devil comes in because God has left you to yourself. Nevertheless, you begin to fancy that God is with you – that you are perfectly justified in your anger. I can tell you what else can happen, too, and this is awful: do not be surprised if at the end of the day you fall into other sins. You may even begin to do things that you never thought you could do. But once the devil gets in you begin to compromise on all sorts of things relating to money, sex and integrity. I knew a man back in Ashland, Kentucky, who eventually fell into sexual immorality. But it began with bitterness. The bitterness may seem a thousand miles from sexual immorality, but this man wouldn't forgive and eventually lapsed into sexual immorality. Why? Because you have been left to yourself.

3 You force God to become your enemy

What causes fights and quarrels among you? Don't they come from your desires that battle within you? You want something but don't get it. You kill and covet, but you cannot have what you want. You quarrel and fight. You do not have, because you do not ask God. When you ask, you do not receive, because you ask with wrong motives, that you may spend what you get on your pleasures. You adulterous people, don't you know that friendship with the world is hatred towards God? Anyone who chooses to be a friend of the world becomes an enemy of God. (James 4:1–4)

The reason God treats you like an enemy is because by not forgiving people you are really saying, 'God, move over; I want to do your job!' *You* are trying to be the judge. You have become judge: you have made a choice to be what God alone is. He is the Righteous Judge. He will do right. He will clear your name. He will punish those who hurt you if that's what they have got coming. He will deal with them; he will expose everything. He feels what you feel. But if you decide to do his work, be becomes *your* enemy. Whenever we judge another, as we will see below, we *never* get away with it. Do not judge and you won't be judged. Judge and you will be judged.

4 You lose your anointing's potential

Because we refuse to forgive, the anointing that God gave is lifted and we become like an empty shell. You may continue for a while because the gifts of God are irrevocable (Rom. 11:29) – even King Saul still prophesied for a while, but eventually he lost everything. Next to being saved, I would regard the anointing as the most precious thing – but one can lose it. We may even flourish for a while; a fallen tree will still have leaves on it at first, but eventually it withers and crumbles. So it is with the anointing. The momentum of other gifts in us may make us think we still have the anointing that we enjoyed yesterday. But mark this down as well: bearing a grudge, trying to punish (God's prerogative), and trying to get even will cut off our anointing. It will be apparent sooner or later – unless we choose to forgive, and to forgive totally.

5 No authentic fellowship with the Father

What we often do in the meantime, when we don't forgive, is to live in a dream world. A person like this is in a deep sleep, and you don't know you are asleep until you wake up. When you wake up you say, 'Oh, I fell asleep!' When you are in a deep sleep you dream things, and when you wake up you think, 'Well I would never do that!' – but you did it in your dreams. So when you are in a deep sleep you do things you wouldn't do if you were awake. I would like this chapter to be a wake-up call. Are you like the prodigal and will come to your senses (Luke 15:17)? As I said at the beginning, it is a no-joke matter: 'If we claim to have fellowship with him yet walk in the darkness, we lie and do not live by the truth' (1 John 1:6).

Jesus thus said, 'If you do not forgive men their sins, your Father will not forgive your sins.' There is, however, something tender in these words: '*Your* Father'. He is still *your* Father, but if you don't forgive, he won't forgive the sins that pertain to your anointing and fellowship with him. That's because he is a jealous God and wants to be first in your life.

When it comes to forgiveness of sins, then, there are two levels. One is what you would call forensic; that refers to what is legal and is the essence of being justified. God legally declares that we are righteous. That is the heart of justification by faith. It is the way God sees us in Christ. But then there is also the spiritual experience, and that is what we must consciously enjoy. We are therefore not only declared righteous, but we are to enjoy a spiritual experience that comes from being forgiven. And you lose that experience when you are in a backslidden state.

Why did Jesus say, 'If you do not forgive men their sins, your father will not forgive your sins'? He said it to motivate us. It's a warning. We all need it. And yet if a person who is not a Christian can be motivated to forgive, even if only in a limited way, how much more should we as Christians be motivated by the Holy Spirit to forgive – totally.

4

Playing God

> Do not judge, or you too will be judged. For in the same way
> you judge others, you will be judged, and with the measure
> you use, it will be measured to you. (Matthew 7:1–2)

I could take you to the very spot – a table in the Duke
Humphrey wing of the Bodleian Library in Oxford. I was in
the process of discovering the great William Perkins (1558–
1602), the Elizabethan Puritan. I came in one day very, very
discouraged, feeling so inferior to the other students at Oxford
University. Here I was from the hills of Kentucky, a place not
particularly known for its academic centres of excellence. The
words 'You don't belong here' came into my mind. It seemed
a very believable suggestion – whereupon my eyes fell on
these words of William Perkins: 'Don't believe the devil, even
when he tells the truth.'

The devil was playing God that day. He loves to play God,
and he wants us to join him in playing God.

Showing graciousness

When Jesus said, 'Be perfect, therefore, as your heavenly Father is perfect' (Matt. 5:48), he was setting the stage for a higher level of perfection than many Christians have looked at. Therefore what we see in Jesus' words, 'Do not judge, or you too will be judged', is an example of this perfection. We cannot expect sinless perfection, but a very high level of maturity is required of us if we want intimacy with God and a greater anointing. To come to the place where you stop pointing the finger is a very high achievement indeed. Matthew 7:1 restates Matthew 5:7, one of the Beatitudes, 'Blessed are the merciful, for they will be shown mercy', because being merciful is showing graciousness. Paul said, 'Let your *gentleness* [my italics] be evident to all' (Phil. 4:5); this derives from a Greek word which literally means being gracious: when you know you could throw the book at somebody but instead choose to be gracious.

Judging is the opposite of graciousness. Graciousness is the consequence of a choice. So remember, at any moment when you are choosing to judge, you are not being gracious. For we *can* stop ourselves and choose to be gracious.

This chapter is an essential ingredient in the process of total forgiveness. Judging and not forgiving are so closely connected that one could almost say that we judge partly because we haven't forgiven. For when we have totally forgiven it is surprising how quickly the temptation to judge is removed.

Judging is uncalled-for criticism. That's what Jesus means by judging. When Jesus says, 'Do not judge', he is not telling us not to notice what is wrong; instead he is saying 'Do not administer any uncalled-for criticism, namely, criticism that is unfair or unjustified.'

Here is an acrostic that I have found helpful, built on the word NEED. When speaking to or about another person, ask yourself if what you are about to say will meet their need:

Necessary – Is it necessary to say this?

Encourage – Will this encourage? Will it make them feel better?

Edify – Will it edify? Will it build them up and make them stronger as a result of what you would say?

Dignify – Will it dignify that person? That's the way Jesus treated other people; he gave them a sense of dignity.

Criticism that is unfair or unjust, *even if it is true*, is not what we should say. The fact that what you might say is true does not make it right to say it. Often Satan's accusations are true; he is an expert at being a judge. The devil loves to play God; he is called 'the accuser of the brothers' (Rev. 12:11). I therefore will never forget William Perkins's words, 'Don't believe the devil, even when he tells the truth.' You may be pointing the finger and telling the truth, but you possibly are an instrument of the devil as you speak.

'To judge' comes from the Greek word *krino*, which basic-ally means 'to make a distinction', something that is generally a good thing to do. Being discriminate can be prudent; it can be wise. The apostle Paul said, 'The spiritual man makes judgments about all things' (1 Cor. 2:15). We are told to make a righteous judgement, but what Jesus is talking about here is judging *people* and making unfair criticisms. It is our way of playing God.

You might be interested to know that I have probably worked on this chapter harder and longer than any other chapter in any book I have written! I began working on it on 22 November 1987. On that evening the Holy Spirit hit me between the eyes and gave me a word in a way that I could not fully explain here even if I tried. It was Luke 6:37 which says, 'Do not judge and you will not be judged.' I made a decision many years ago to read Luke 6:37 every day. I still do – every single day. Even though I have it memorised, I turn to it and read it, because sometimes a verse – though memorised – has a deeper effect when read. If you ask, 'Why do you read it every day?' then I would anwer that it is because judging is probably my greatest weakness.

However, I have chosen Matthew 7:1ff. for this book because Jesus goes into more detail here. Jesus gave us these verses for exactly the same reason that he warned us about not forgiving: it grieves the Holy Spirit.

Judging like this is almost always counter-productive. So when I judge I may think, 'What I want to do is change this person, straighten this person out.' Yet it has the opposite effect almost every time! Sooner or later it backfires. It offends the other person; it doesn't really help. Jesus therefore gave us these words partly so that we might see that judging is almost always counter-productive.

The degree to which we resist the temptation to judge will be the degree to which we ourselves are largely spared of being judged: 'Do not judge, or you too will be judged.' In Matthew 7:1 it is given as a fair warning, but in Luke 6:37 it is put as an actual promise: 'Do not judge, and you will not be judged. Do not condemn, and you will not be condemned. Forgive, and you will be forgiven' (Luke 6:37).

Being critical of others

Avoid dishing out criticism, then, and you will escape being criticised. Being judged is painful, whether it is totally untrue or totally true. When we are criticised, we don't like it; it is painful, it hurts. It is harder to say which is more painful, to be falsely accused or to be accused when it is true. We don't like it either way.

Jesus treats our tendency to judge by appealing again to our self-interest. But this should not surprise us; God often does this. He motivates us with the idea of what's in it for us if we do it, and what's in it for us if we don't. Therefore Jesus helps us right at the beginning, using the Greek word *hina* which means 'purpose'. It is often translated 'in order that', and this is implied in the Authorised Version translation: 'Judge not, that ye be not judged.' The meaning is, 'Judge not, in order that you too will not be judged.'

So what Jesus has done for us is give us a pragmatic reason not to judge. In other words, if you don't like being judged, then stop judging. This obviously and immediately appeals to our self-interest.

This is the best way to make friends. Dale Carnegie's book *How to Win Friends and Influence People* is largely based on the teachings of Jesus (even if he took the fruit without the root) and he brought them into immense practical teaching. It is partly based upon the Sermon on the Mount. It is not a Christian book and Dale Carnegie managed to keep godliness out of it, but one can still see the good that would come by living this way.

We don't like being judged. As Somerset Maugham once said, 'When people ask for criticism they really want praise.' Before you read this very book, you can be sure that my close friends will have seen it first. And while I may well appreciate their kind words, I *feel* I must have their criticisms. But they will hurt a bit – for we all love praise!

God *could* 'throw the book' at me at any time. But maybe he *won't* throw the book at me, until he sees me pointing the finger at somebody else. God says, 'Sorry about this, R.T., but I must step in and deal with you. You should know better.' God himself will see that I get judged.

It is so easy to criticise. You do not need to read a book on how to develop your ability to point the finger. You do not need more education, a high IQ; you do not need a lot of experience to be good at it, and judging is certainly no sign that you are more spiritual. It has often been said that a little bit of learning is a dangerous thing. Sometimes a little bit of spirituality is a dangerous thing because one may be just spiritual enough to see what is wrong – and you want to point the finger. And yet you are not spiritual enough *not* to point the finger! It is so easy to judge. It flows *not* from the depth of our spirituality, but it flows from a fault in our walk with Christ. You may say, 'Well, I have got to say something or nobody else will!' What if the latter is true? They still don't want to hear it, we are not really helping. They will feel worse and yet we keep on doing it. Jesus' word is a practical command. 'Stop it!' says Jesus. What matters to God is pointing the finger:

> If you do away with the yoke of oppression,
> with the pointing finger and malicious talk,
> and if you spend yourselves on behalf of the hungry

and satisfy the needs of the oppressed,
then your light will rise in the darkness,
and your night will become like the noonday.

(Isaiah 58:9–10)

What may motivate us not to judge is this: consider the pleasant atmosphere you live in when it is devoid of criticism. How good and pleasant it is when we all live in harmony! (Ps. 133:1.) It is so sweet, it is so good. Then consider the pain that follows from being critical. So if you don't like being criticised, don't criticise! I don't say we will never be criticised, but we can be spared a lot of grief by tongue control.

Speaking blessings emerges from these words: 'Let your conversation be always full of grace, seasoned with salt, so that you may know how to answer everyone' (Col. 4:6), and 'Do not repay evil with evil or insult with insult, but with blessing, because to this you were called so that you may inherit a blessing' (1 Pet. 3:9). Jesus even said, 'But I tell you that men will have to give account on the day of judgment for every careless word they have spoken' (Matt. 12:36). That is enough to scare me to death!

Uncalled-for criticism calls for a defensive reaction that usually leads to a counter-charge. So if I judge you for this, you will immediately say, 'Yeah, but what about you? I saw you do this; I heard you say that!' 'Oh no I did not!' 'Oh yes you did!' It is almost always counter-productive. It also gets God's attention. Today's English Version translates this verse, 'Do not judge others so that *God* will not judge you', because that is precisely what Jesus is teaching. It is God who will do the judging. Your immediate judge may well be that other person who will retort back, but *that* may be God at work even then, letting them have a go at you.

According to Jesus, this painful consequence is just. For if somebody judges us because we judged them, we are getting what we deserve. They may not have deserved what we gave them, but we deserve what they have given us back which only came about because of a lack of tongue control on our part.

There are two levels of motivation for applying Jesus' words, 'Do not judge or you too will be judged.' The first level is the lower level – self-interest. Jesus actually appeals to the lower level, because he appeals to our self-interest. So it is not bad to be motivated by this, because Jesus encouraged it. But there is a higher level too: you avoid grieving the Holy Spirit. When we grieve the Spirit we lose presence of mind, clear thinking, and we may lose self-control. All hell may therefore break loose: 'The tongue also is a fire, a world of evil among the parts of the body. It corrupts the whole person, sets the whole course of his life on fire, and is itself set on fire by hell' (Jas. 3:6). All because of that one judgmental comment.

So the lower level of motivation is: spare yourself unnecessary trouble. The higher level is: don't grieve the Holy Spirit so that you can have continual communion with him, flow in the Spirit, walk in the Spirit. It is the greatest feeling in the world.

None of this is saying that we must *never* criticise, as we will see in more detail below. It depends on what our spirit is, what is behind it. The judging Jesus warns against is *unjust criticism*. Therefore Jesus is not calling us to put our critical faculties in suspension. It has to do with attitude.

Jealousy

It is so often nothing but jealousy, as well as an unforgiving spirit, that cries out to have another person put in their place. Here we are talking about the essence of jealousy: we want another person to have their come-uppance. We want to be able to say, 'I told you so!' So why do we judge and mete out uncalled-for criticism? Possibly because we resent the fact that this person isn't seen as they should be. They are popular and they don't deserve to be popular. We resent it that they are admired. They shouldn't be liked – if people only knew them!

A few years ago Rob Parsons, executive director of Care for the Family, was in a deep crisis. He was as low as he had ever been. It was a Sunday morning, and he heard a knock at his door. There stood David Pawson, who said to Rob: 'This too will pass, and the truth is worse than what they know.' Profound words.

Remember that what is true about you and what is true about me is actually worse than what they know! But God knows. And the moment we point the finger at another person we may hastily think, 'They got what was coming to them.'

So if you want to invite God to become involved in your life, he will. But not in a very happy manner in this case, for at the very moment you point the finger at the other person, God says, 'Hmm. Now I have some work to do.' He may well go for *you* – not them – for doing the judging. That is the way it is. That is what Jesus is saying. So if I resent it that another person gets away with something and is not being punished, it's because I am jealous that they are being given mercy when they ought to get justice.

Jealousy is the hardest thing on earth to see in oneself. I

can see it in you, but not in me! We will deny it for as long as we can. We wouldn't want to admit to a fault like that; we wouldn't want to admit to such insecurity. So we deny it. But it is only a matter of time before we will see it. We may not see it today or tomorrow, but one day we will see the real reason why we point the finger: jealousy, resentment over another person getting away with something; that they are admired; that they are not getting the come-uppance they deserve and are not found out.

Jealousy sometimes springs from the fear that a person won't get justice. We all want mercy for ourselves, but justice for others!

Nathan and David

The reason we want to judge another person is usually because it involves us; we have got annoyed and worked up, and we become emotionally involved. But we can also just hear about something that irks us – which appeals to our self-righteousness – and be equally emotionally involved. That is what happened when Nathan the prophet came to David.

David, two years before, had committed adultery and murder. But Nathan didn't go to David the day after Bathsheba became pregnant or the week after Uriah the Hittite was killed. So, because he hadn't been caught for two years, David probably thought, 'I'm not going to get into trouble over that one!' Then, unexpectedly, out of the blue, here comes Nathan the prophet: 'David, I need to say something to you!'

'Nathan, come in!' said David. 'Come in!'

Nathan gives a parable and then he comes to the punch line: 'Now a traveller came to the rich man, but the rich man refrained from taking one of his own sheep or cattle to prepare a meal for the traveller who had come to him. Instead, he took the ewe lamb that belonged to the poor man and prepared it for the one who had come to him' (2 Sam. 12:4).

David burned with anger and pronounced sentence on this gross injustice. The angels also listened. The sentence was, 'As surely as the LORD lives' – that's strong language, that's taking the oath – 'the man who did this deserves to die! He must pay for that lamb four times over, because he did such a thing and had no pity' (2 Sam. 12:5–6).

Nathan said, 'David, you are the man!'

Well, that is what happens. David couldn't stand the thought that this traveller would be given the ewe lamb of the poor man and that the rich man would not get justice, so he said that the rich man must get justice, and this was his decree. He did not know that in that moment he pronounced a sentence on himself, and the very matter of withholding mercy back-fired on David so that justice is exactly what he got. Nathan went on to show that David had just pronounced his own sentence as well: 'Now, therefore, the sword shall never depart from your house' (2 Sam. 12:10). That is what Jesus is saying to us.

Judging is God's prerogative

Judging people is elbowing in on God's exclusive territory and this is something he will not tolerate. Deuteronomy 32:35 is quoted twice in the New Testament: 'It is mine to avenge; I will repay' (Rom. 12:19; Heb. 10:30). That means, *you* don't do it. 'That's my privilege,' says God. Judging is God's prerogative; it is nobody else's. Once we move in on his territory God looks at us and says, 'Really?' We are the ones who then get judged, not the people we judged! Even if we should succeed in exposing that person by bringing them down, or if we cause them to lose face, or make them feel horrible and awful and they finally admit, 'Yes, it's true, it's true, I'm sorry, I'm sorry!' we may think we have won the battle. But God will win the war and judge us. It is only a matter of time.

What Jesus means is that to move in on the territory of the Eternal Judge is to get his attention, and we do not want to get his attention in this way. Jesus gives us the principle, a very simple principle: with the measure you judge will be the way it will be applied. In the same way as we judge others, we will be judged; the measure we use will be measured to us.

Being a judge is an aspect of God's character that you and I are not allowed to imitate. The word 'godliness' means 'being like God'. You say, 'Well, I am going to be judge then — he's judge and I'll be judge.' Not so. That is *not* what God means when he says he wants us to be like him. There *are* certain aspects of God's character where we are commanded to be like him. For example, 'Be holy, because I am holy' (1 Pet. 1:16). We are commanded to live holy lives. 'Be merciful, just as your Father is merciful' (Luke 6:36). And we are commanded not to judge, but to show mercy. God wants us to walk in integrity. He wants us to walk in truth and sincerity. But there is an aspect of the character of God where there is *no trespassing allowed*, and the moment we cross over and begin to point the finger, we err. For example, if I refer to another person's faults, or past, or do something to make them feel guilty, the person that I am addressing isn't going to get anything like what I am going to get for doing it.

If you and I are foolish enough to administer uncalled-for criticism, then remember three things: God is listening; he knows the truth about *us*, and he is ruthlessly fair. As Malachi says, 'Then those who feared the LORD talked with each other, and the LORD listened and heard. A scroll of remembrance was written in his presence concerning those who feared the LORD and honoured his name' (Mal. 3:16). I used to hear on the radio a quartet singing every Sunday morning from the Fuller Tabernacle in Long Beach, California:

> He hears all you say;
> He sees all you do;
> My Lord is writing all the time.

Never forget that God knows the truth about us: 'Nothing in all creation is hidden from God's sight. Everything is uncovered and laid bare before the eyes of him to whom we must give account' (Heb. 4:13). How would you like it if, as you are pointing the finger at somebody, an angel from heaven showed up right on the spot and said, 'Stop! Here's what I know about *you*', and then called out what is knowable about you to the person you were judging? God could do just that, because the whole time you are speaking God is looking down from heaven, and the angels are also looking and saying, 'I can't believe he or she would talk to that person like that, because we know so much about *him* (or her)!'

David forgot for a moment what he had done. Then Nathan came to him. We too may begin to think, 'All is well', and 'I am wanting to serve the Lord', and we forget what we are really like. But God is gracious. He may still use us, and then one day decide to judge us if there is no genuine repentance. The fact that he is using any of us doesn't mean we are perfect.

Who knows what God will yet show me about myself that I haven't even thought of – or have even forgotten? God knows everything about us. He has enough on us to bury us. As I said, we all have skeletons in the cupboard, and God knows every one of them, most of which we may have forgotten. The audacity we have in judging another person when God knows so much about us! He doesn't like it. He knows what we have thought; he knows what we have done; he knows what we have said.

Here are two practical verses which we all would do well to take on board:

> Do not pay attention to every word people say,
> or you may hear your servant cursing you.
>
> (Ecclesiastes 7:21)

> Do not revile the king even in your thoughts,
> or curse the rich in your bedroom,
> because a bird of the air may carry your words,
> and a bird on the wing may report what you say.
>
> (Ecclesiastes 10:20)

God has a way of getting us exposed, caught and found out just when we thought, 'There is no way that could happen to me.' When does it happen? It is a promise from the Lord that equitable judgement will be administered. The word 'equitable' means what is fair, what is just. All of God's judgements are ruthlessly fair. One day we will all stand before the judgement seat of Christ and for once in human history there will be fair judgement. Not a day passes when we don't hear of a court letting someone off and we say, 'Where is the justice?' But the way God obtains justice is stunning. The question is, is it here in this present life or is it in the life to come? The ancient Greek Church Father Chrysostom said it is in the life to come. For Paul said, 'For we must all appear before the judgment seat of Christ, that each one may receive what is due to him for the things done while in the body, whether good or bad' (2 Cor. 5:10). 'You, then, why do you judge your brother? Or why do you look down on your brother? For we will all stand before God's judgment seat' (Rom. 14:10).

On the other hand, God does deal with people in this present life if they are saved. Paul said in 1 Corinthians 11:30: 'That is why many among you are weak and sick, and a number of you have fallen asleep.' The point is, God doesn't always wait to the final judgement. God can choose any day of the year and make it a day of judgement.

Perhaps you have said, 'Well, I have got away with this!' Perhaps it could be that God closed his eyes to it. It *is* possible, since he has not dealt with us after our sins nor rewarded us according to our iniquities (Ps. 103:10). But on the other hand, it could be that God is so angry that he has decided to wait. God is the opposite of us. At least, he is the opposite of me. Speaking personally, I find the angrier I get the sooner I deal with it. With God, the angrier he gets, the longer he waits.

But why does God do it? What's it all for? Because God is for the victim; that is a theme that runs through the whole Bible. God blesses those who are for the underdog, and will judge those who neglect the underdog.

5

When we are right to judge

Why do you look at the speck of sawdust in your brother's eye and pay no attention to the plank in your own eye? How can you say to your brother, 'Let me take the speck out of your eye,' when all the time there is a plank in your own eye? You hypocrite, first take the plank out of your own eye, and then you will see clearly to remove the speck from your brother's eye. (Matthew 7:3–5)

The purpose of this chapter is to examine the possibility that we *should* make an attempt to help correct someone's behaviour. Having given us strong language in Matthew 7:1, 'Do not judge, or you too will be judged', one could conclude that there must *never* be a situation in which we make a judgement regarding another. But this is not quite the case. Jesus leaves the door ajar, even if it is only just ajar, when he says, 'First take the plank out of your own eye, and then you will see clearly to remove the speck from your brother's eye.' This verse, looked at carefully, *does* provide a loophole for judging – in some cases.

There is a reason for this. Sometimes it is absolutely right to warn a person about someone. For example, John the apostle, who has so much to say about loving one another, warned about a troublemaker in the church (3 John 9–10). Paul had to report that Demas forsook him because he 'loved this world', Alexander the metalworker caused real harm, but Paul added: 'May it not be held against them', referring to all who had deserted him (2 Tim. 4:9–10).

When it is right to correct behaviour

Why is this chapter important? Not because there are exceptions to the rule, but because it is sometimes unjust for the world generally and the church in particular that certain people are at large who can do great harm. This is why a person who is raped should testify in court; it is why a person who threatens the unity of the church should be dealt with. There are many types of cases that could be mentioned, but what we shall do in this chapter is to show the basic principles that must be followed and that are to be carried out without violating the spirit of the seven principles of total forgiveness.

Facing our own faults first

Jesus introduced this matter of having to administer justice with a question: 'Why do you look at the speck of sawdust in your brother's eye and pay no attention to the plank in your own eye?' (Matt. 7:3). Since Jesus addressed this to the church, it should not surprise us that so many of our quarrels come from within the family of God. This is why the reference is to 'your brother's eye', meaning one's spiritual brother or sister –

not one's natural kin. This verse shows so candidly how we tend to let small things in the other person upset us – the 'speck of dust' – and so easily overlook the big, negative things in our own lives: the 'plank'. This lack of objectivity about ourselves disqualifies us from being helpful. It is a vital ingredient in the matter of being qualified to judge. When we lose objectivity about ourselves, seeing only the speck of dust in others but not the plank in our own eyes, we must render ourselves out of order to sort out another person.

Fault-finding, then, is out of order. Jesus' rhetorical question, 'Why do you look at the speck of sawdust in your brother's eye and pay no attention to the plank in your own eye?' is about meddling over what 'gets our goat'. The fault we see is what Jesus calls a speck. That annoys us, but the whole time we don't see our own very serious problem. This shows no objectivity about oneself whatsoever. For the cause of fault-finding, or meddling, is the plank in our own eye which we cannot see. 'Plank' is Jesus' word for what is wrong with us; it is sin in us, evidence of our fallen nature. It is what makes us so eager to point the finger rather than to forgive.

The plank in us causes 'poor eyesight'; it magnifies the speck of dust in the other person but also simultaneously blinds us to our own faults! The plank in us focuses on and magnifies the weakness in the other person so that it appears to us much worse than it really is. But it is really our own weakness that is in operation: simultaneously magnifying (their faults) and blinding ourselves (to our own faults).

Jesus wants us to see that we have a worse problem than the other person does when we are critical and point the finger. The very act of fault-finding is worse than the fault we think we see in the other. Therefore before Jesus provides this tiny loophole by which we can make a correction in another person, he wants to establish the criterion for making that correction; when we lose objectivity about ourselves we remove ourselves from being qualified judges. For if we truly see the plank in our own eye – thus having objectivity about ourselves – we will not be gazing with agitation at the speck in the other person's eye.

The question therefore follows: is the fault-finding the plank in our eye, or is the plank some other sin in our life? The answer is: it is both.

Jesus elaborates on this when he asks, 'How can you say to your brother, "Let me take the speck out of your eye," when all the time there is a plank in your own eye?' (Matt. 7:4.) The purpose of this direct question is to wake us up and show how disqualified we are to judge when our own house isn't in order. For the basic cause of fault-finding is the plank in our own eye. When Jesus asks, 'How can you . . . ?' no doubt some would reply: 'I'll show you!' But he is assuming we are rational, sensible people who would immediately see through the inconsistency of meddling in another's affairs. He thus assures that we will see the unreasonableness of meddling.

The assumption therefore is this, as we will see: if we had no plank in our own eye it would not be unreasonable to offer help. But when we have the plank and still meddle, our fault is far worse than theirs. Meddling is always uninvited and almost always unwelcome.

How to behave if someone criticises us

What if, by the way, someone meddles in *your* life? What should be the response? First, maintain a sweet spirit. Never forget, 'A gentle answer turns away wrath, but a harsh word stirs up anger' (Prov. 15:1). Secondly, agree with them. It never hurts to do this. Usually there is a little bit of truth in what a critic will say to us or about us. You can always say, 'I see what you mean.' Thirdly, thank them. This will not only defuse them if they are annoyed, but will also enable them to save face should they be up to no good. That way, we haven't made an enemy unnecessarily in the process. What we must never do when being confronted like this is to defend ourselves or try to impress on others how good or right we are; and never punish. Never get even. Never make them look bad. Ask them to pray for you! But say it in a non-combatant manner. Never say it sarcastically. Say it sincerely, 'I need all the help I can get.' In the meantime you can always pray for them. But don't tell them this; it will annoy them. The principles of total forgiveness should enable us to make friends, not lose them.

Jesus will not allow us to play God. He is the ultimate judge and we must be extremely careful not to trespass into his territory. It may be recalled also that the judging that Jesus prohibits is *unfair criticism*. Jesus now says we are hypocrites if we engage in this kind of judging: 'You hypocrite, first take the plank out of your own eye, and then you will see clearly to remove the speck from your brother's eye' (Matt. 7:5).

Times when we *are* permitted to judge

We come now to the 'loophole', for I see it as judging – with divine approval – in one sense. The word 'loophole' normally refers to a way of evading a rule or contract, especially through an omission or inexact wording of its provisions. However, in this case it is Jesus who both lays down the rules and also provides the loophole – with exact wording.

But is Jesus telling us that we are qualified to judge after all? Yes, sometimes. We have seen that the plank in our eye disqualifies us from judging since it blinds us to our own faults and magnifies the defect in another. On the other hand, should we succeed in obliterating this plank, then apparently we are set free to remove the speck from another's eye.

However, there is an obvious question: does Jesus start out by saying, 'Do not judge, or you too will be judged' (Matt. 7:1), and then finish by saying, 'First take the plank out of your own eye', and then you can judge after all – with certain conditions attached?

We must be careful here. Some people with absolutely no objectivity about themselves will claim to be qualified judges on the premise that they have no plank! I have actually met people who can look you in the eye with a straight face and claim the right to judge because they got rid of their plank years ago!

In other words, say some, all you have to do in order to qualify as judge is to say, 'I have no plank in my eye; therefore I am qualified to sort you out.' And if you question them, *you* will be accused of judging!

Am I to believe that Jesus is encouraging some to judge on the basis that they no longer have a plank in their eye? If so, we are back to square one; we can all go back to pointing the finger on the grounds that we have removed the plank!

We are now at what is arguably the most delicate stage of this book. Why? Because we all face unjust situations every day. The issue is, how long do you tolerate wrong? Surely, though, people will take unfair advantage of this 'loophole'. And yet there is a feeling in your bones that somebody must speak out. But we are told not to judge. We are told to forgive. Jesus went so far as to say, 'But I tell you, Do not resist an evil person. If someone strikes you on the right cheek, turn to him the other also' (Matt. 5:39).

So surely we can never judge?

According to Matthew 7:5 we can apparently judge another if we have no plank. But who is bold enough to say that he or she has no plank? I am certainly not! When I read Jeremiah 17:9 I find that it is an apt depiction of me, 'The heart is deceitful above all things and beyond cure. Who can understand it?' When Paul says that there is no good thing in his flesh (Rom. 7:18), I have to say, 'That's me too.' When he says, 'Here is a trustworthy saying that deserves full acceptance: Christ Jesus came into the world to save sinners – of whom I am the worst' (1 Tim. 1:15), I am sometimes inclined to say, 'That may have been true then but now surely I am the worst.' Therefore if I have to know there is no plank in me before I can offer any sort of correction in another, or warn about a person I feel is evil, I will have to say here and now I am out of the picture! I will not be among those qualified to judge.

Matthew 7:5 is surely saying at least one of three things: (1) no one ever gets rid of the plank, therefore no one can judge; (2) one can get rid of the plank and then – and then only – can you help another; or (3) there is a way forward when one focuses on his or her *own* plank, and self-effacingly offers correction to another in a way that will be welcomed.

What is our Lord's purpose in these words? He wants to help us in different and difficult situations. We could carry out the principle of total forgiveness to such an extent that we let all rapists, child abusers and murderers out of prison so that they could roam the streets and do more damage. We could allow carnal Christians (yes, they do exist – 1 Cor.

3:1ff.) to take over a church and destroy it if we take the principle of total forgiveness without understanding Jesus in Matthew 7:5.

Jesus wants to promote honesty. Admit you are unqualified as a judge as long as there is a plank. We all have a plank in our eye.

Jesus also wants to promote humility. It would be the height of arrogance to claim we have got rid of the plank. This would be tantamount to claiming to be without sin. But John said, 'If we claim to be without sin, we deceive ourselves and the truth is not in us' (1 John 1:8).

The main thing Jesus wants is to offer help and a way forward. Please note: Jesus never says we should not help another. He never says we should not see what is there, for the very next verse in the Sermon on the Mount assumes we must be discriminating: 'Do not give dogs what is sacred; do not throw your pearls to pigs. If you do, they may trample them under their feet, and then turn and tear you to pieces' (Matt. 7:6). Later in Matthew, Jesus says:

> If your brother sins against you, go and show him his fault, just between the two of you. If he listens to you, you have won your brother over. But if he will not listen, take one or two others along, so that 'every matter may be established by the testimony of two or three witnesses.' If he refuses to listen to them, tell it to the church; and if he refuses to listen even to the church, treat him as you would a pagan or a tax collector. (Matthew 18:15–17)

Perhaps the most relevant verse in the New Testament is when Paul says, 'Brothers, if someone is caught in a sin, you who are spiritual should restore him gently. But watch yourself, or you also may be tempted' (Gal. 6:1).

I conclude that in Matthew 7:5 ('You hypocrite, first take the plank out of your own eye, and then you will see clearly to remove the speck from your brother's eye') our Lord is promoting honesty and humility, but is none the less offering help in situations where things go wrong. There are situations every day where something needs to happen, such as somebody speaking out. In the light of the New Testament verse quoted above we must surely conclude that Jesus is saying that sometimes there needs to be someone who must step in and offer help; it would be irresponsible not to do so. There is therefore a way forward and a way whereby we can truly help to remove, delicately, the speck from our brother's or sister's eye without meddling.

A close look at Jesus' words shows the order of priority: 'First, take the plank out of your own eye.' What we are required to do *first* is to admit to the plank and weep. If you and I want to help a person in need, or speak up against injustice, our first priority is to get it right in ourselves. This does not mean extracting a defect as a dentist removes a bad tooth (if only it were that simple!); it means humbly and soberly admitting to our own weakness. That is a step towards having some objectivity about ourselves. We have all sinned.

I believe also that Jesus is putting before us, quite ostensibly, a paradox. For example, how would we ever obliterate or remove the plank? We can't. Is this Jesus' tongue-in-cheek way of saying that we can never help a person with a fault because we can never remove that plank in our eye? No. Is Jesus teaching sinless perfectionism to which few can attain, therefore they and they only are qualified to help people with faults? No.

Nobody removes the plank in his or her own eye absolutely.

If we could remove the plank absolutely then we would be sinless – and even qualified to do God's own job! The truth is, no one ever removes the plank in an absolute sense. Jesus is not saying that the removal of the plank is possible in a total and complete sense; that would lead to self-righteousness flourishing more than ever. People everywhere would claim the right to point the finger.

Removing our plank in a limited way

But it is, I believe, possible to remove the plank in a limited way. For example, take Galatians 6:1: 'Brothers, if someone is caught in a sin, you who are spiritual should restore him gently. But watch yourself, or you also may be tempted.' Let us say that I have found a brother who has fallen into the sin of adultery. He not only has lusted (which would be adultery in the heart according to Matthew 5:28), but has actually slept with a woman who is not his wife. I feel that someone must approach him. Am I qualified? In an absolute sense, no – because I am a sinner too. As a matter of fact, perhaps I can see myself doing what he has done – but for God's grace. Yet because I am *not* in an adulterous relationship, I therefore *have* removed this particular plank from my eye in a sense. The reason I might be qualified to help is because I am not going to be fault-finding. I will let him know that I too could do the same thing. This does not mean that I will necessarily turn him around, but he may not resent my coming to him or see me as meddling. He will know I am concerned for his own life and spiritual state, not to mention the honour of God's name.

A few years ago two elders had the task of approaching a man in their church who was in an adulterous relationship.

On their way to the man's home one elder said to the other, 'Do you believe that you too could fall into this sin?' The reply: 'No.' The elder who asked the question then said, 'You are not qualified to go in and approach this man' – and the visit was cancelled. For the essential qualification is the spirit required by Paul in Galatians 6:1: 'Brothers, if someone is caught in a sin, you who are spiritual should restore him gently. But watch yourself, or you also may be tempted.' The person who knows full well that he or she could do the very same thing – but for the grace of God – is the only person qualified to help a fallen Christian.

This then is why I believe we can remove the plank in a limited way. We cannot do it absolutely but perhaps we can do it approximately: enough that we can see ourselves as sinners, but not as committing the exact same sin we are trying to correct.

There is a rule of thumb: the one who is hardest on himself or herself will probably be gentle with others. Those who are most aware of their own weaknesses are more likely to help others. The one who doesn't moralise, but instead encourages, is the one most qualified to engage in the ministry of reconciliation and restoration. For those who want to help in a non-judgmental way know all too well that they have a plank and are aware of their own weaknesses. These people are more likely to succeed when others fail; They are more likely to be welcomed when the meddler will be unwelcome.

Things that follow when we have dealt with our plank

These things will follow when one has dealt with one's own plank in the ways suggested:

The person attempting to help another, will avoid being emotionally involved, which means that he or she has no personal axe to grind. They are not agitated or inwardly churned up; self-esteem does not come into it.

When Jesus asks us to remove the plank from our eye he is really telling us that we should disqualify ourselves when we get upset with the person who has a speck! We are qualified to help another person only to the extent that we truly love and care and are not annoyed by them. Once we are emotionally upset, we disqualify ourselves from being the one who might help.

When there is a judgmental spirit, or unfair criticism, bitterness is not far away. It will be recalled that the chief way we grieve the Spirit is by bitterness. This is why Jesus said, 'remove the plank'; more often than not, there is bitterness at bottom when we try to put somebody straight. If there is *no bitterness*, we may be able to help.

For this reason it is often a person who is disconnected to the situation who is best able to help. I do not say that this is the only person who can help, for total forgiveness means an absence of bitterness and the one who has totally forgiven may be very helpful indeed. But it will be a person who is not personally involved who can remove, delicately, a speck of dust from another's eye.

This person, moreover, will be sympathetically detached. That means there is sympathy without any prejudice or emotional involvement. Any professional – lawyer, doctor, scholar or clergyman – must maintain a sympathetic detachment in their work. The lawyer is sympathetic with all clients, but not personally involved to the extent that he or she loses sleep. The minister or doctor is sympathetic towards the one who calls on their expertise, but is never so wound up that he or she cannot give a rational judgement.

To be sympathetically detached means that you care about the person you want to help, but that you are not fixated or obsessed with that person. A person who has a serious sexual weakness, for example, will almost certainly not be able to help the person who comes to them with the same problem. Removing the plank means that you can actually help that person because you are sympathetic and you are not going to superimpose your hang-ups on them.

Any counselling worth its salt will be led by one who is both sympathetic and detached. Sometimes marriage counselling is the only way forward because a husband and wife may be neither sympathetic to the other nor detached, but instead up to their ears in 'emotional baggage'. In other words, impartiality is necessary for a counsellor to help with a marriage in difficulty.

The person qualified to remove the speck of dust, then, is impartial. That means that he or she will not be moralising, making the person feel guilty, or perhaps feel governed by some personal interest. The only consideration will be the honour of God's name.

A person who is neutral but compassionate will probably be welcomed – and also be effective. This is why I will not be able to help you with your problems if I am annoyed that you have a problem in this or that area. My being annoyed means I must pass up the opportunity to help you. I wouldn't be able to help you.

Jesus never tells us how to remove the plank from our own eye, possibly because such a removal is not possible in the absolute sense. But paying sufficient attention to our own plank will help to keep us from pointing the finger or meddling; neither do we violate the words of Jesus that opened this discussion: 'Do not judge, or you too will be judged' (Matt. 7:1).

When we *can't* help another

To sum up, I believe that there are some objective principles that summarise what Jesus meant regarding situations when it is right to judge and situations when it is wrong. You rule yourself out when:

1 your nose is out of joint because something or someone makes you cross. In other words, when you are churned up, stay out;
2 you are personally or emotionally involved, even though there is an injustice – unless, of course, you have been *asked* to testify or give opinions;
3 your desire is to punish or get even;
4 there is envy or jealousy;
5 your own self-esteem is connected to the matter in question.

When we *can* help another

You are able to help when:

1 you are meeting a need – remember the acrostic NEED earlier in the book (p. 93);
2 you would be irresponsible not to speak, or it is inappropriate not to get involved because you are in a strategic position to help;
3 you have been asked to step in by a responsible person who has no 'agenda';

4 you are utterly impartial and have no agitation or feeling of being annoyed;

5 nothing matters to you more than the honour of God. But be careful – many use this as their justification. One day you will find out whether it really was God's honour you cared about – or just yours!

6

The art of forgiving ourselves and forgetting

If we confess our sins, he is faithful and just and will forgive us our sins and purify us from all unrighteousness. (1 John 1:9)

The love chapter of the Bible, 1 Corinthians 13, is a perfect demonstration of the cause and effect of total forgiveness. The high-water mark of this wonderful passage is that phrase in verse 5: love 'keeps no record of wrongs'. The Greek word with the negative participle is *logezetai*, which means not to reckon or impute. This word is important to Paul's doctrine of justification by faith. For the person who believes, such faith is 'credited' as righteousness (Rom. 4:5), the same Greek word as in 1 Corinthians 13:5. It is put the other way around in Romans 4:8, again using the same word: 'Blessed is the man whose sin the Lord will never count against him.' Therefore *not* to reckon, impute or 'count' someone's wrongs is to do for that person what God does for us: namely, not recognising his or her sin. In God's sight their sin no longer exists. So too with us when we totally forgive.

The dangers of keeping a record of wrongs

We are acknowledging here that evil took place; you obviously see the evil, but you erase it. Before it becomes lodged in your heart, the wrong thing the person did must be wilfully forgotten. This way, resentment does not have an opportunity to set in. If however, it has already set in and become lodged in the heart, the way forward is the same: one must *stop* keeping records! The love described in 1 Corinthians 13 comes by total forgiveness. That means tearing up the records!

Keeping no record of wrongs, then, is both preventive medicine as well as a cure. If one can overlook the evil at the outset, he or she is prevented from bitterness. But if bitterness is there one must attempt to destroy the record of wrongs so that the hurt can never be thrown up again.

Satan knows what we know and he hangs around day and night to exploit any such weakness. He will take advantage of any weakness in us if he can. The failing he loves to see in us most of all is the inability to forgive and the tendency to point the finger. It is in the context of offering forgiveness that Paul said that he was not ignorant of Satan's ways (2 Cor. 2:11). The chief way Satan takes advantage of us is through our bitterness – refusing to let something drop but instead to keep dwelling on it. It is therefore crucial that we get rid of bitterness lest we hand the devil an invitation on a silver platter to move in on us and control us. He will certainly do that if we aren't very careful. It is dangerous to keep a record of wrongs.

Why do we keep records? To use them. Why do we keep records of wrongs? To refer to them. 'I'll remember that,' we say – and we are true to our word. And it usually comes up sooner rather than later. We use the record of wrongs to call attention to them and, mostly, to punish. We often punish others by bestowing the pain of guilt. Although we may acknowledge with our minds God's words, 'It is mine to avenge' (Rom. 12:19), we really say in our hearts, 'God isn't doing his job.' So we do God's job by punishing the person who hurt us – whether it be a spouse, a relative, a church leader, old school teacher, or the insensitive and nasty boss.

Letting go of a record of wrongs

Love is a choice; it is an act of the will. Keeping a record of wrongs is also an act of the will, although one comes by it quite naturally; *not* keeping a record of wrongs will always be the result of a conscious act of the will.

The key to letting go of that record, and therefore the key to total forgiveness, is also tongue control. It is what we say that causes the forest fire to which James refers:

Likewise the tongue is a small part of the body, but it makes great boasts. Consider what a great forest is set on fire by a small spark. The tongue also is a fire, a world of evil among the parts of the body. It corrupts the whole person, sets the whole course of his life on fire, and is itself set on fire by hell. (James 3:5–6)

The irony is that, instead of getting something off your chest by pointing to their evil, it not only causes the uncontrollable fire to erupt, but also the poison that remains inside us. Instead of that poison disappearing, it doubles, intensifies and gets a thousand times worse in the end. It is but a satanic victory. It began with the tongue, yes; but it is ultimately traceable to keeping a record of wrongs.

How does one deal with the tongue? Two things, I believe, will help: (1) refuse to point out the wrong *to* the person, and (2) refuse to point out the wrong *of* the person when that person is not around. Were this to become a chosen lifestyle the record of wrongs might also disintegrate! In other words, by refusing to bring up the hurt, the record of that hurt will disappear in the sense that it eats you up all the time.

This sort of thing can happen in imaginary conversations. It is when you can't get 'what they did' off your mind and you fantasise as to what you might say to them, or do to them, and what you might tell another. This conversation may go on and on – and a whole hour has passed when you neither got any work done nor felt any better!

One evening at about eleven o'clock, as I was going to bed, I found myself having an imaginary conversation about someone. I imagined I had an opportunity to spill the beans about this person. I pictured the scenario in which I made myself look good and the other person look bad. But the Holy Spirit – miraculously – got into the matter. I felt I heard him say, 'You can get a victory right now if you refuse to think anything in order to clear your name.' Even though it was but a conversation that existed only in my own mind, I realised that I had an opportunity to triumph – in my spirit! It was a wonderful moment. It was pivotal. Because it was as if it was *real* – and I refused to say anything at all about the person. A peace entered my heart, and I knew then and there that I must never again enter into imaginary conversations – unless it meant refusing to vindicate myself. I would not recommend you to engage in an imaginary conversation. But for those who find the practice therapeutic, I would only say let your thoughts be positive and wholesome; keep no records of wrongs in your *thoughts* and you will be less likely to expose such records by your *words*.

When I am tempted to say something negative but refuse to speak, I can often feel the release of the Holy Spirit within. It is as if God says, 'Well done.' It is a very good feeling. After all, Jesus is touched with our weaknesses (Heb. 4:15), and equally he lets us feel his joy when we overcome them! He rewards us with an incredible peace; he sends the Spirit to witness.

Refusing to keep a record of our *rights*!

The logical conclusion of not keeping a record of wrongs, though, is equally a refusal to keep a record of your own *rights*! It is just as dishonouring to God's grace to keep a record of rights as it is to keep a record of wrongs. Why? Because it is exalting yourself and implicitly saying, 'I told you so' – making someone else look bad. It takes a spiritual giant not to say, 'I told you so.' We may say, 'I don't want to say it', but really we *do* want to say it!

Quite a few people not only keep a record of wrongs, but have an even longer list of how often they have been right! We want people to know how right we are. We want them to know that we said it first: 'Do you see how right I was?' 'You should have listened to me.'

Love not only tears up a record of wrongs, but also a list of rights. That way you have destroyed the record you would have used to vindicate yourself! If there is no record of rights lodged firmly in your head, you will not be able to refer to it to prove how right you were. Therefore forget what they did that was wrong, forget what you did that was right. This is partly why Paul said, 'I do not even judge myself' (1 Cor. 4:3). I have often concluded that few deserve the vindication they think they are entitled to. I can only say that if vindication is truly deserved, then that vindication will surely come.

Jim Bakker's experience of letting go of wrongs

I recently watched an extraordinary edition of *Larry King Live* on Cable News Network. This was the first time in fifteen years that Jim Bakker and Tammy Faye Messner (formerly Tammy Faye Bakker) had appeared on television together before the eyes of millions. Jim Bakker, the television evangelist, had been sentenced to forty-five years in prison for something, it turned out, he did not do. His supposed crime was deliberately misleading his television viewers to send in money to buy homes for them that did not exist. Jim was not vindicated for a long time, but in the meantime his wife Tammy Faye divorced him and married his best friend, Roe Messner. After being out of prison for five years, Jim married his present wife, Lori Beth. Larry King invited the *four* of them to be on his television show.

Each had a story to tell – of deep, deep hurts and total forgiveness. Both Jim and Tammy, before Jim's imprisonment, felt betrayed by an American minister who was almost entirely responsible for Jim being sentenced to prison. Both needed to forgive this minister. Tammy had to forgive Jim for his sexual encounter with a young lady – the episode that led to his downfall. Jim not only had to forgive the unjust witnesses and biased judge who sentenced him but also his wife for marrying his best friend while he was in prison. This is to say nothing about certain hurts that the other two participants – Roe and Lori Beth – had experienced.

Larry King asked Jim how it felt. Jim replied, 'We were in a situation that was unbelievable. I was to be in prison for forty-five years. At my age I would never have gotten out of prison before I died. And so I don't blame Tammy Faye for going on with her life.'

Not that Jim felt that way at first! But slowly he came to terms with things and totally forgave Tammy Faye and fully appreciated her decision. He continued:

Nelson Mandela says that he didn't look at prison as a down; he took it as an up. When you suddenly find yourself in prison for forty-five years – my theology didn't allow for that at that time. It was like God had walked away from me. And I know millions of people have gone through experiences saying, 'Why, God?' And as I studied the word of God and I had time to move into the Bible it was my faith in God and God renewed my faith. My faith was actually growing after five years. It was the greatest training and seminary and intimate relationship with God that I ever had.

Larry King then asked, 'Are you saying, in a sense, in retrospect, it was good that you were in prison?' Jim replied, 'Absolutely, absolutely! I learned so much, and now working in inner cities all over the world I understand the people. When I say I've been in prison it's, like, better than being ordained. They respond to me because they know I'm like them.'

Larry turned to Tammy: 'You could help a lot of people because there's a lot of it in the news now, the Juliano story and the Clinton story. You were able to forgive and to overcome the worst thing a wife can go through. How were you able to do that?' Tammy answered: 'Forgiveness is a choice. Our whole lives are choices.'

Larry then said to Tammy Faye, regarding Jim's affair, 'You could have been bitter.' She replied, 'I could have chosen to be bitter and hate him or I could have chosen to forgive. It was very hard for me to forgive him, it was very hard. But . . . I was able to forgive him and understand what happened and go on.'

Larry turned to Jim again: 'And how did you feel about the forgiveness?' Jim replied:

The Bible is so clear, and this is what I studied in prison. When I began to study the words of Jesus Christ, and he said if you don't forgive from the heart, forgiving everyone, you will not be forgiven. Christ said, 'Blessed are the merciful for they shall obtain mercy.' I needed mercy, I needed forgiveness, so I wanted to give out to others what I needed.

Larry asked Jim, 'Did you feel terrific that she was able to forgive this?' Jim answered:

Whether she forgave me or not, you know, I had to forgive her, I had to forgive everyone. I mean, everyone who goes through divorce, it's painful, and I took all the blame finally because I realised all the mistakes that I had made. I realised I had the affair; I am the one who screwed up and I left her out there by herself to literally face dying without a husband.

Larry then said to Tammy: 'So you're friendly now. How do

you explain that?' Tammy replied, 'I like this man, he's a really nice man. We were married for thirty years and we've had wonderful memories together and we had two awesome kids together, and I like him.'

Larry asked Jim if he prayed for Roe. He answered: 'Absolutely . . . I pray for Roe. I had to really forgive Roe for marrying my wife at that point in prison. I mean, you have to forgive. I'm in prison and God was dealing with me to forgive everybody. You can't just forgive, you've got to pray for God to bless your enemies.'

Larry responded, 'It doesn't make it easy, does it?' Jim then said:

I had to come to the point where I had to literally tell God – Roe's one of the greatest builders in the world – and I had to say to God, if God you want me to ever build something again, I would build it with Roe Messner. And I had come to that point where I could say, God, your will be done, not my will be done.

Larry then looked at all four and asked: 'There's no jealousy in this room?' The unanimous answer: 'No.'

'Do you say that you're all friends?' asked Larry. The unanimous answer: 'Yes.'

'How do you explain that?' asked Larry King.

Jim Bakker stepped in:

Only God can help people truly forgive and go on. In the book of Colossians it talks about that. Because of what Christ did, we are pure, we are without judgement on ourselves. When I first went to prison I was even questioning, 'Where, God? Where are you?' But as I went through the months of studying the word of God I realised that prison was God's favour. God is saying, 'I want you to come aside.' Everybody in the Bible, from Genesis to Revelation, has either been in a pit or a prison or the backside of the desert. They've all been through bad things. So bad things happen to people – they happened to all the great men of God.

Larry King then concluded that part of the interview and echoed what millions watching must have thought: 'I'm amazed,' he said.

As we have seen, Jim Bakker was eventually vindicated. A professor of law at Fordham University stepped in out of the blue and took on Jim's case, and showed convincingly that Bakker was totally innocent of the charges of fraud. After five years in prison, Jim was released. He went to live in solitude for a long while on a farm in North Carolina. His biggest problem, he says, was *forgiving himself*. He never believed for a moment that he was guilty of financial dishonesty, but knew he had erred in at least two areas: (1) his affair, and (2) his prosperity teaching (that God wants everybody to be prosperous). In these, he knew he was wrong. How could he forgive himself?

Forgiving ourselves

We now come to an important matter to which I promised to return: forgiving ourselves. It is at this point that I fear I could be writing beyond my own experience. When it comes to forgiving others, I *think* I have made some progress – for otherwise I could not write this book. But I fear I would be edging close to being hypocritical if I were to look you in the eye and say, 'I have forgiven myself too.' I *think* I have, but cannot be sure.

Forgiving ourselves means experiencing the love that keeps no record of our *own* wrongs. This love is a choice, as we have seen, and to cross over to the place where we choose to forgive ourselves is no small step.

It is therefore one thing to have the breakthrough regarding others – totally forgiving them by destroying the record of information; it is quite another to experience what for some may be an even greater breakthrough: totally forgiving ourselves. So many say: 'I can forgive others, but I can't forgive myself. I know God forgives me, but I can't forgive myself.'

One of the problems I have in forgiving myself is the tendency to forget that this too is a life-long commitment. In precisely the same way that I must forgive others every single day – which is why I read Luke 6:37 daily – I must do this with myself.

Let me restate why we daily have to forgive those who hurt us and why it is a life-long commitment. It is because (1) we are so often made to re-live what they did, (2) we feel not a little irked that they are still getting away with it, and (3) Satan moves in to exploit our weakness in this area. This is why we must *renew* our commitment to forgive – and make sure we haven't pasted back together those torn-up bits of paper that recorded the wrongs done to us. It is literally a daily process in many cases.

So too with forgiving ourselves. We may wake up each day with the awareness of past mistakes and failures – and wish so ardently that we could turn the clock back and start all over again. We may then have feelings of guilt that we *are* off the hook for our stupidity. But the enemy, the devil, loves to move in and take advantage of our guilt. For that reason, forgiving ourselves is as much a life-long commitment – for those of us who have the problem – as forgiving an enemy or an unfair person.

This chapter just might bring about the breakthrough you have been looking for. It could set you free in a way never before experienced. This is because we have been afraid to forgive ourselves. We cling to fear as if it were a thing of value. The truth is, this kind of fear is no friend but instead a fierce enemy. The very breath of Satan is behind the fear of forgiving ourselves. We don't trust what we might be like if we forgave ourselves. In much the same way, we fear what others would be like if they felt totally forgiven – abuse it – so we are afraid of it in ourselves.

When God sets us free, he puts us on our honour to set others free too. When we pass on this forgiveness to others, we must likewise put them on their honour.

Jesus knows that many of us have this problem. This is a further reason why Jesus turned up unexpectedly after his resurrection when, behind closed doors, the disciples were assembled both in terror and also ridden with guilt. Jesus not only wanted them to know they were totally forgiven; he wanted them to forgive themselves. Instead of reminding them of what they had done, he assumed that nothing whatever had happened and said, 'As the Father has sent me, I am sending you' (John 20:21). This gave them dignity. It showed that nothing had occurred that might change Jesus' plans and strategy for them. He had already sent a signal to Peter, who denied knowing Jesus, when the angel said, 'But go, tell his disciples and Peter, "He is going ahead of you into Galilee. There you will see him, just as he told you" ' (Mark 16:7). And yet all of them had 'deserted him and fled' (Matt. 26:56).

They felt utterly unworthy. Then the risen Lord showed up and assured them of a future ministry!

I have often thought that one of the reasons Peter was so effective on the Day of Pentecost is that he was aware of having been forgiven. He knew full well that fifty days before he had denied knowing Jesus to a little servant girl! He could never forget that look on Jesus' face when the rooster crowed and Peter 'went outside and wept bitterly' (Luke 22:61–2). It was a real antidote to self-righteousness. When he preached on the Day of Pentecost, he felt utterly forgiven, and also knew he was in no position to preach to his fellow Jews with even a touch of smugness and condescension. Knowing he was a forgiven sinner also stopped Peter from competing with God's glory on that day. Only God could have the glory for those 3,000 conversions.

I can't prove that Peter had totally forgiven himself, but I suspect that he had done so. I well remember one Sunday morning just before the eleven o'clock service when I had had an argument with Louise. I should never have done it, but I slammed the door of our flat, went down in the lift – and before I knew it I was bowing my head on the upper platform at Westminster Chapel before several hundred people. I don't know what they were thinking, but I know what I was thinking: 'I should not be here. I have no right to be here. Lord, how on earth could you use me today? I am not fit to be in this pulpit.' It was too late to send a note to Louise saying, 'I'm sorry.' I wasn't able to get her attention. I could only ask God for mercy and try my best to forget myself. I assumed I was about to make the biggest flop in preaching in the history of Westminster Chapel. Never in my life had I felt so unworthy. But when I stood to preach I was not prepared for the help I got. God simply undergirded me and enabled me to preach as well as I'd ever done! That is partly why I think Peter did so well on the Day of Pentecost. When we are emptied of self-righteousness and pride we enable God to move in and act through us.

Signs that we haven't forgiven ourselves

The proof that we *haven't* forgiven ourselves is that we still feel guilty, blame ourselves, and cannot function effortlessly even though we have confessed our sinfulness to God. If we feel guilty, blame ourselves, and find that we cannot function normally – even though we have confessed our sins to God – it indicates that we haven't yet totally forgiven ourselves. It means we are hanging on to guilt that God has washed away; refusing to enjoy what God has freely done. But 1 John 1:9 is either true or it isn't: 'If we confess our sins, he is faithful and just and will forgive us our sins and purify us from all unrighteousness.' If we have confessed our sins we must take this promise with both hands – and forgive ourselves, which is precisely what God *wants* us to do.

The person who hasn't forgiven himself or herself is an unhappy person. The result of not forgiving oneself is often that we can't forgive others. It is, at times, like the old question: which comes first – the chicken or the egg? In much the same way, my not forgiving myself will backfire – and I struggle to forgive others. Or my not forgiving others may result in a great sense of shame by my not forgiving myself. People who can't forgive others are often so ashamed of themselves that they repress their guilt and strike out at other people. The irony is, the degree to which we forgive others will often be the degree to which we forgive ourselves; the degree to which we set ourselves free will often be the degree to which we forgive others. But it is not always as simple as that, although there is much here that we must all ponder. It is almost certainly true that he or she who is ridden with guilt will be an expert in sending others on a 'guilt trip'.

It is sometimes almost impossible to say which comes first: forgiving others so you will be able to forgive yourself, or forgiving yourself so you will be able to forgive others. But it is not *total* forgiveness until both are equally true.

Why can't we forgive ourselves?

What is the cause of our inability to forgive ourselves? At the end of the day, why don't we forgive ourselves?

It may be anger. This is why Joseph said to his brothers, 'And now, do not be distressed and do not be angry with yourselves for selling me here, because it was to save lives that God sent me ahead of you' (Gen. 45:5). These brothers were beginning to get the message that Joseph had forgiven them, but Joseph knew they would struggle with forgiving themselves. One of the proofs that Joseph had totally forgiven them was that he didn't want them to be angry with themselves.

That is the way God forgives; he doesn't want us to be angry with ourselves. Joseph, it may be recalled, is considered to be an Old Testament type of Christ, that is, one who in some ways is like Jesus before Jesus himself appeared on the scene. In the exact manner that Joseph forgave his brothers, so does Jesus forgive us; and as Joseph did not want them to be angry with themselves, so does Jesus not want us to be angry with ourselves.

Not forgiving ourselves is self-hate; it is being angry with ourselves. We hate ourselves for what we have done. Those men Joseph forgave hated themselves for what they had done twenty-two years before: selling their brother to the Ishmaelites to be a slave. They could not turn the clock back. They could not get a second chance.

Jesus says to you and me: 'Don't be angry with yourself.' He will even give us a way of saving face: that God was behind all that has happened; that it was within God's general purpose in what he wants to do with our lives. Peter was none the worse for his folly of denying Jesus. He felt so ashamed, yes, but I suspect he was easier to live with after that!

I remember talking with a minister who told me about a sexual affair of another preacher. He went on and on about how disgusting and reprehensible this man's behaviour had been. He wanted my opinion on what should be done. I said, 'Tell nobody else, just pray for this man.' 'Really?' said this minister, who wanted me to enter into his feeling of disgust. Again I said, 'Say nothing.' 'Really?' said this man once more. 'Yes,' I said, 'It could happen to you. Try administering the spirit put to us in Galatians 6:1: "Brothers, if someone is caught in a sin, you who are spiritual should restore him gently. But watch yourself, or you also may be tempted." ' I remember feeling a little uncomfortable with this man. I said to myself, 'If I ever fall into deep sin of any shape or form, this is the last man I would ever tell.'

But that is not the end of the story. A few years later the same minister came to me with a problem: he had become attracted to a woman in his congregation. I immediately recalled the aforementioned conversation, but said nothing about it. I simply urged this man to break this thing off – utterly and immediately. Thankfully, he put an end to the attraction and continued to preach. He confessed to God and felt forgiven. But there is more: his preaching after that was more tender and his general spirit was one of graciousness, not self-righteousness.

Nobody needs to have an affair – or even come close to it – in order to get over self-righteousness. In fact, I have known some who became even more self-righteous after falling into sin: they tried to justify everything they had done. But the answer to self-righteousness is not found by looking for an opportunity to sin. Don't be a fool. However, what *is* true is this: God will take one's sinful past and make it work together for good so brilliantly and beautifully that you are tempted to say that this is the way it was supposed to be! Of course, it *wasn't* supposed to be this way. Not at all! But it *seemed* that way. Why? God meant it for good. And one fringe benefit of being a returning backslider is that there should be no room for a self-righteous attitude.

So you still can't forgive yourself? Is it because you are angry with yourself? Jesus says to you at this precise moment: 'Please don't be. Don't be angry with yourself.' He will begin today to cause all that has happened to fit into a pattern for good if you forgive yourself. And don't feel guilty in doing so! God says, 'Take your forgiveness and don't look back.' God will take the wasted years and make them look good before it is all over. It is like Joel promised, 'I will repay you for the years the locusts have eaten' (Joel 2:25).

In some cases, though, it is *fear* more than anger that militates against our forgiving ourselves. Regret over the past leads to guilt, and guilt often leads to fear. There is the fear of missing 'what might have been', the fear that what has happened cannot *possibly* turn out for good.

True guilt and pseudo guilt

There are in fact two kinds of guilt: true guilt (sin against God) and pseudo guilt (when sin is not really in the picture). When we have sinned – as Joseph's brothers did, and as Peter and the disciples did – we must confess it to God (1 John 1:9). The blood of Jesus takes care of true guilt. For that blood basically does two things: (1) it washes away our sin – as though it never had existed, and (2) it perfectly satisfies God's eternal justice. God is looking only to his Son's precious blood for satisfaction. Therefore any chastening or disciplining that comes from our Father is not adding to Jesus' blood. He is not getting even with us; he 'got even', if you like, at the cross. The Greek word that translates as 'chastening' or 'disciplining' (Heb. 12:6ff.) means *enforced learning*. It is when God teaches us a lesson and makes sure that we learn it! Whereas disciplining is necessary because we are sinners, it does not follow that God is looking for more satisfaction. For this reason, sin that is confessed to God (because you are sorry) is to be taken as being totally forgiven by him. Any guilt we feel beyond that is pseudo guilt.

There are, however, two kinds of pseudo guilt: (1) when sin was never involved in the first place, and (2) where sin has been forgiven. In the matter of feeling guilt, it must be acknowledged that pseudo guilt – though false – is very real; that is, we feel acutely guilty. But it must be called pseudo guilt because, when it is thought through, there is *no good reason* for feeling guilty.

Take, for example, when you are involved in an accident. If you are driving a car and a child runs out in front of you at the very last second and is knocked down, the guilt can be overwhelming. But there was no sin. It doesn't need to be confessed to God. (Providing, of course, you weren't driving carelessly or too fast.)

Another example of false guilt is missing out on an opportunity. I have a friend in Florida who had a chance to buy a property many years ago for $5,000. He turned down the offer, and today that property is worth over a million dollars. He feels guilty that he didn't use his money more wisely, but this is not true guilt.

The list is endless as to how pseudo guilt can affect our lives for ill. We can become weighed down by something that we had nothing to do with; accused of not speaking to a person when you didn't even see them; not answering a letter you never received. These are not sins, but they *can* make us feel guilty.

The other kind of pseudo guilt is when you confess your sins – have even repented deeply – but don't *feel* forgiven. Once we have acknowledged our sin, we need to accept our forgiveness and leave the rest to God.

I have not hidden very well over the years my sense of failure as a father. I now wish I had given more time to T.R. and Melissa in those early years at Westminster Chapel. I now believe that putting them first – not my church or sermon preparation – would have resulted in the Chapel carrying on just as well, if not better. But it's too late now. For me to feel guilty over this is not pleasing to God because he has totally forgiven me. He wants me to accept my forgiveness (I believe it was a sin to put my church and ministry before my family) and let *him* restore the years the locusts have eaten. If therefore I let myself dwell on my failure I am giving in to pseudo guilt – yet sinning when I do so because I am dignifying unbelief. It is therefore required of me to keep destroying the record of my wrongs – every single day.

One of the main reasons why God doesn't like it when we don't forgive ourselves is because it is a subtle way of competing with Christ's atonement. God punished Jesus for what we did (2 Cor. 5:17). When we don't accept our own forgiveness, it is probably because we want to punish ourselves. Instead of accepting that the Lord laid on Jesus all my iniquity (Isa. 53:6), I want to punish myself for my failures. It is competing with Christ's finest hour. God doesn't like that.

Fear and not forgiving ourselves

Fear, is one of the main reasons why we do not forgive ourselves. He or she who fears has not been made perfect in love, and fear 'has to do with punishment' (1 John 4:18). One of the derivatives of fear is punishing ourselves by not forgiving ourselves. We feel it would be wrong for us to escape with our folly unpunished, so we punish ourselves. This is wrong. It is not what God wants at all. In fact, said Paul, 'For you did not receive a spirit that makes you a slave again to fear, but you received the Spirit of sonship. And by him we cry, "*Abba*, Father" ' (Rom. 8:15). Paul said to Timothy: 'For God did not give us a spirit of timidity, but a spirit of power, of love and of self-discipline' (2 Tim. 1:7).

When we realise that fear – and punishing ourselves for our mistakes – displeases God, this should result in an ever-increasing sadness for not forgiving ourselves. We are required to walk away from our past folly. And when we are tempted to look back, try to see that sign that says 'No trespassing allowed'. Or, as Corrie ten Boom put it, 'No fishing allowed'.

My wife Louise was greatly blessed by the ministry of Rodney Howard-Browne, especially when she attended a week of his services in Lakeland, Florida, in January 1995. But it was not only Rodney's ministry that helped Louise; it was the singing ministry of Janny Grein and her song:

> As the seasons make their turn
> There's a lesson here to learn
> Broken wings take time to mend
> Before they learn to fly again
> On the breath of God they'll soar
> And be stronger than before.
>
> Don't look back into the past
> What was fire now is ash
> Let it all be dead and gone
> The time is now for moving on.
>
> (Janny Grein)

Louise remembers Janny shouting out these words: 'Let the past be past – at last.'

That is what God is saying to us in this chapter. Let the past be past at last. Forgive ourselves as well as those who have damaged us.

Pride, self-righteousness and self-pity

What we have been saying in this chapter about not forgiving ourselves may be, at the end of the day, traceable to *pride*. That is what is fundamentally at work when we compete with the blood of Christ. We in our arrogance and self-righteousness cannot bear the Lord doing everything for us so graciously, so we think we are being clever if we help him out a bit. It is an abominable way to think. Our pride must be eclipsed by the humility to let God be God and the blood of Christ do what it in fact did: remove our guilt and satisfy God.

As fear and pride are like identical twins, so are self-righteousness and self-pity. We feel sorry for ourselves and show it by not forgiving ourselves. It is for this reason that pseudo guilt can develop into very real and heinous guilt before God. It is false guilt for God has said, 'You're not guilty', but we make it real guilt when we in effect reply, 'Yes we are'.

The bottom line is: not forgiving ourselves is wrong and dishonouring to God.

But let us assume at this stage that you read this and say, 'I agree. I know not forgiving myself is wrong, but I just can't help it.' What can be done to help you forgive yourself if you truly want to? The problem is partly psychological, partly theological. I shall not attempt to be a psychologist in this book. That expertise lies outside my anointing. But nevertheless I do believe that there are some psychological problems that can be healed in part by solid and sound theology.

Understanding guilt

The ability to forgive ourselves comes partly from understanding guilt. Guilt means feeling that one is to blame. For example, when you blame others, you have kept a record of their wrongs. When you blame yourself, you have kept a record of your wrongs. True guilt is where sin is involved. The Holy Spirit shows us our sin. The initial work of the Spirit according to John 16:8 is that he convicts of sin. When Isaiah saw the glory of the Lord he was convicted of sin (Isa. 6:1–5). When we walk in the light we know the blood cleanses of sin; but walking in the light also reveals sin in us that we may not have seen before (1 John 1:7–8).

But the sense of guilt that God instigates is temporary; it is momentary: 'For his anger lasts only a moment, but his favour lasts a lifetime; weeping may remain for a night, but rejoicing comes with the morning' (Ps. 30:5). God only uses guilt to get our attention. When we say, 'I'm sorry' (because we mean it), that's enough for God. He doesn't beat us black and blue and require us to go on a thirty-day fast to supplement Christ's atonement. He convicts us of sin to get our attention; but having done that, he wants us to go forward.

Understanding grace

The ability to forgive ourselves therefore extends to understanding grace. Grace is undeserved favour. Mercy is not getting what we do deserve (justice); grace is getting what we don't deserve (total forgiveness). The need in us to feel and be deserving before we can move on is pride – self-righteousness. Grace isn't grace if we have to be good enough for it to apply to us.

Peter *knew* what he had done and knew he was forgiven. David *knew* what he had done and pleaded for God's mercy (Ps. 51). Grace is accepting what we don't deserve; it may feel so unfair when we have been so horrible. We have let God down; let others down.

But it *is* fair, says John: 'If we confess our sins, he is faithful and just and will forgive us our sins and purify us from all unrighteousness' (1 John 1:9). The blood of Jesus did a wonderful job. God is not looking for further satisfaction. We forgive ourselves to the degree we really do believe that!

It comes down to this: our understanding of God. God is gracious. He doesn't want us to feel guilty. He knows our frame. He knows how we are formed, and remembers that we are 'dust' (Ps. 103:14).

There is nothing more tormenting than guilt, but God's love drives away fear. The closer we are to God, the less fear there is. The further we are from God, the more fear there is. Because God is *love* (1 John 4:16); he is *good* (Ps. 136:1).

God's style is this: he shows us our sin in order that we will acknowledge it, and not justify it but instead confess it – so that we might move on and let the past be past. It is the devil, never God, who accuses from then on (Rev. 12:11). As we have seen, when we won't forgive ourselves we become an easy target for Satan. He looks with glee when he sees a Christian who can't forgive himself or herself; he will exploit that weakness to the hilt. But he has a tough time with the person who has truly forgiven himself or herself for all that is past.

All accusations regarding confessed sin come from the devil. When you know you have applied 1 John 1:9, and you sense an accusing voice over that past failure, mark it down: that voice did not come from your heavenly Father. It did not come from Jesus. It did not come from the Holy Spirit. It came from your enemy the devil, who works either as a roaring lion – to scare (1 Pet. 5:8) – or as an angel of light – to deceive (2 Cor. 11:14) – or sometimes both simultaneously. And never forget, perfect love casts out fear (1 John 4:18).

One of the dangers of not forgiving ourselves is that we will not only let fear control us, but we may even lapse into the trap of remembering others' wrongs. In other words, having totally forgiven others, but not ourselves, will lead us back into bitterness towards others. And we have seen how counter-productive bitterness towards others is – but it is also counter-productive when we are bitter towards ourselves.

Let the past be past

The sweet consequence of not keeping a record of wrongs (theirs and ours) is that we let go of the past and its effect on the present. In this way, we cast our care on God and rely on him to restore the wasted years and to make everything turn out for good. We find ourselves, almost miraculously, accepting ourselves as we are – which God does. With all our failures – as God does. And even accepting ourselves, while still knowing we have the potential to make more mistakes. God never gets disillusioned with us; he loves us and knows us inside out already. That's why he can still use us.

Moses had a past; he was a murderer. Years later he would proclaim the eighth commandment: you shall not murder (Exod. 20:13). David had a past, and a future after his shame: 'Then I will teach transgressors your ways, and sinners will turn back to you' (Ps. 51:13). Jonah deliberately ran from God, but was still used in an astonishing Revival (Jonah 3). Peter's disgrace – denying Jesus – did not abort God's plans for him. All these men had to forgive themselves.

Can you do that? Having forgiven others, it is time to forgive yourself. Even if that sin takes so long to forgive. But once you have done it, forgive yourself as well. That is exactly what God wants of you and me. It is long overdue: let the past be past . . . at last.

7

How to forgive – totally

> But I tell you: Love your enemies and pray for those who
> persecute you. (Matthew 5:44)

Not all those we must forgive are enemies, for there are those
we must forgive who either do not know they have hurt us
or, if they do, would not have done so intentionally. We must
forgive anyone for whom we feel anger because it is we not
they who are in need. And it is for this reason that total
forgiveness – in a sense – becomes a selfish thing. As Jim
Bakker said, 'Christ said, "Blessed are the merciful for they
will be shown mercy." I needed mercy, I needed forgiveness,
so I wanted to give out to others what I needed.'

Forgiving those who are *not* enemies

Some of the people I have had to forgive the most were not
enemies at all. By this I mean that they were not trying to
bring me down or hurt me. They were people I had hoped

would help me. On one occasion I asked an old friend to write a commendation for a book I had written. He refused, partly because there wasn't enough in it he agreed with, and partly because I was getting a reputation for mixing with people he didn't approve of. This hurt. He was certainly no enemy, but I still had to forgive him. I have had to forgive those who felt a need to distance themselves from me because I don't echo their 'party line'. I have had to forgive those who no longer need me as they once did. These things hurt. But such people are not enemies. The irony is that it is sometimes harder to forgive those who are not enemies, but have hurt you deeply, than it is to forgive one who is indeed an enemy.

I do believe I have had some enemies. By this I mean those who were not only opposed to me and my teaching, but actively sought to bring me down and destroy my reputation. I have had to forgive them – totally – and I believe by the grace of God I truly have.

What do we mean by having an enemy?

What is an enemy? This is a person who either wants to harm you, or who would say something about you so as to call your credibility or integrity into question. They would rejoice at your downfall or lack of success. They would not pray that God will bless you and prosper you but sincerely hope that God will bring you down.

An enemy is a person who hates you, but would not always admit to the word *hate*. I say that because, should your enemy be a Christian, they know it is wrong to hate. So they will use any other word or words: 'loathe', 'despise', 'can't stand them', 'they make me sick', 'can't bear the sight of then'. In a word: they just don't like you and will show it in one way or another sooner or later. Jealousy is often part of the picture. But if that person is a Christian, then here again, don't expect them to admit to being jealous! 'Me? Jealous? Never!'

An enemy is also a person who will take unfair advantage of you. To quote Matthew 5:44 in the Authorised Version, they 'despitefully use you'. They walk over you. If they know you live by the principle 'It is mine to avenge' (meaning that God vindicates without our aid), then instead of respecting this they will exploit it all the more – knowing that you will not retaliate. Sometimes a Christian will be unscrupulous in business with another Christian because they know this particular Christian would never take another Christian to court (1 Cor. 6:1–8). They may say libellous things in print because they know you will not sue.

An enemy will often persecute. The Greek word for 'to persecute' simply means 'to follow' or 'to pursue'. They pursue you because they are obsessed with you. King Saul became jealous of David because the latter was more popular. The result was that King Saul was more worried about the threat of David's anointing than he was of Israel's arch-enemy – the Philistines! Saul pursued David but never succeeded.

The persecutor's main tactic is to discredit you if you are likely to stay in the picture. They will put the record straight where you are concerned. They will say things to your boss, keep you from getting that promotion or pay rise; they will tell your friends things that they feel need to be told lest you get away with them. They will go out of their way to keep you from succeeding, from being admired by the people in the office or church. What is more – if they are Christians – they claim they are doing it for God and his glory! 'They will put you out of the synagogue; in fact, a time is coming when anyone who kills you will think he is offering a service to

God' (John 16:2). People like this don't kill with the sword or a gun; they do it with the tongue or pen. Perhaps sometimes you wish they would just kill you physically and get it over with!

The blessing of having an enemy!

But the greater the hurt, the greater the blessing that will come. The chief motivation to forgive is not only the promise of mercy by being merciful, but the greater reward that is promised – whether it be bestowed here on earth or in heaven. I say that because of Jesus' words when he came to the ultimate Beatitude:

> Blessed are you when people insult you, persecute you and falsely say all kinds of evil against you because of me. Rejoice and be glad, because great is your reward in heaven, for in the same way they persecuted the prophets who were before you. (Matthew 5:11–12)

If you have a real, relentless, genuine enemy – and you are sure that this person is not a figment of your anxiety or imagination – you should see yourself as sitting on a mine of twenty-four carat gold. Except for the fact that all enemies of Christ are ours as well, not everybody has a fierce enemy. Not everybody is that blessed. But if you are so blessed – and Jesus saves the best for last in the Beatitudes – grasp the opportunity with both hands. You should (in your mind) take this person's picture, enlarge and frame it, and thank God every time you look at it. Your enemy, should you handle him or her correctly, will turn out to be the best thing that ever happened to you.

I was saying to my wife Louise, as I was preparing to write

this chapter, that the incident that led to my having to forgive those who hurt me those many years ago was 'the best thing that ever happened to me'. I said that to her because it's the truth. Well, perhaps that is a *slight* exaggeration when I think of my conversion, marrying Louise, and one or two other good things! But that is often the way I feel; I wouldn't take *anything* in exchange for the devastating incident that led Josif Tson to say, 'R.T., you must totally forgive them.'

> When through the deep waters I cause thee to go,
> My rivers of woe shall not thee overflow;
> For I will be with thee, thy troubles to bless,
> And sanctify to thee thy deepest distress.
>
> 'K' in Rippon's *Selection*, 1787

When you know that a person is obsessed with you and is out to discredit you, you are very, very blessed indeed. This doesn't happen to everybody. You are chosen, for behind your enemy is the hand of God. God has raised up your enemy – possibly just for you! King Saul's pursuing of David was the best thing that could have happened to David at the time. It was part – a most vital part – of David's preparation to be king. He had the anointing without the crown (1 Sam. 16:13) and God was ensuring that when the day came when he wore the crown, he would be ready. Remember the quote of Dr Lloyd-Jones: 'The worst thing that can happen to a man is to succeed before he is ready.' God did David a very special favour: he raised up Saul to keep him on his toes, to teach him to be sensitive to the Spirit (1 Sam. 24:5) and to teach him total forgiveness. Saul was David's passport to a greater anointing.

Totally forgiving our enemies

When you totally forgive your enemy you have crossed over into the supernatural. Perhaps you are like me in that you wish you could excel in all the gifts of the Spirit; you wish you could have a hand in signs and wonders; you'd love to see your usefulness intensified and extended by a double anointing – for that sort of thing is *supernatural*, that is, it is 'above' or 'beyond' the natural order of things. In other words, there is no natural explanation for the truly miraculous. But if you and I totally forgive one who is truly an enemy (as I described above), believe me, you have just crossed over into the realm of the supernatural. You may not speak in tongues; you may not have raised a person from the dead. But when you totally forgive an authentic enemy, you are *there*: you have made it into the Big League, the supernatural.

I believe we are talking about the highest level of spirituality that exists. This is as good as it gets. Totally forgiving an enemy is as spectacular as any miracle. No one may even know, though. You quietly intercede for them in solitude. Only God, the angels and the devil know.

We are talking about a feat greater than climbing Mount Everest, for totally forgiving an enemy is to climb the spiritual Everest. It means the highest watermark in anyone's spiritual pilgrimage.

And yet it is within reach of any of us. No high connections in government, business or society are required. No particular cultural background is needed. No amount of A-levels or university education is needed. A high level of intelligence is not required. You and I can do something exceedingly rare: forgive an enemy (if we have one). Loving an enemy defies a natural explanation.

It begins with having sufficient motivation. I am literally seeking to motivate you in these lines to do what very few do – but which all *can* do: totally forgive anyone who has hurt you. And the blessing is beyond words to describe.

Why do I have enemies?

When Jesus said, 'Love your enemies', he assumed that we have one or more. Most people do to some degree. Sadly, many (if not most) will be from within the community of faith. Certainly Jesus assumed this. Nothing has really changed. So much persecution comes from those who claim to believe in God as much as you do. And yet the issue may not be theological at all. They simply don't like *you*!

The origin of such enmity may be explained almost entirely in terms of the *flesh*. For example, your enemies cannot cope with you being as you are. They will never admit to that of course, just as they will not admit to jealousy. These people are ridden with guilt and take it out on you.

It may be that they cannot cope with your being on the particular side you are on. If you were on their side or supporting their party line, well – just maybe – they would tolerate you. But if you happen to be on the side of a different group that they can't abide, you simply get caught in the crossfire! It is no fault of your own.

They might be angry with God for blessing you. Or for putting you where you are. You have that prestigious job. It pays well. You are admired by your boss and people in the office. God has blessed you with certain talents and gifts. There will always be someone who will try to bring you down. If you have been blessed with a good reputation, do not be surprised if someone resents it that God could possibly be behind this. Very often, your enemy doesn't know that he or she is really angry with God.

Whereas a good case can be made that the origin of your enemy is the devil (see John 13:2) as well as the flesh, the ultimate reason you and I have an enemy is *God*. Why? It is what we need. David needed an enemy. So do you and I. It helps to humble us lest we take ourselves too seriously. An enemy shows us what we are like. Frequently God will allow an enemy to make a broadside attack on us – and then God appears to desert us. He did this with Hezekiah in order to test him and see what was in his heart (2 Chron. 32:31). God raises up an enemy to see if we really want to be like Jesus.

So don't be angry with your enemy! It is often God who is the one behind that person who wants to keep you from reaching your goals. 'But doesn't God want me to reach my goal?' Yes. If that goal is his idea. 'Delight yourself in the LORD and he will give you the desires of your heart' (Ps. 37:4). If your goal stays the same the more you love God, than it may be a good sign that you will reach it – in his time. God will exalt you in due time (1 Pet. 5:6). God designs an enemy to keep us on our toes, but also on our knees. God knows exactly what we need. He is sovereign. He will keep our enemy alive and well as long as we need them. Whether your enemy is temporary or a 'life sentence', never forget that God is at the bottom of it all.

I was recently preaching in Northern Ireland where a minister came up to me afterwards and asked, 'Can your wife be your enemy?' That one took me back a bit. But I said, 'Yes.' I believe that in a marriage a husband and wife can develop such a dislike for each other that the only way forward for that marriage is Jesus' teaching on total forgiveness. Someone once said to the saintly John Fletcher, 'Did you know that

John Wesley gets up every morning at four o'clock to pray?' Fletcher replied, 'And do you have any idea what it must be like to live with Mrs Wesley?' All that can be said about an enemy generally may describe one's husband or wife. The only way forward is to forgive. Totally.

Your enemy's objective is to punish in some way. To put you in your place. To keep you checked. They feel that if they don't do this, it won't be done. Rather than let God do it, they feel they are God's very instrument in putting you in your place. Whereas their motive at bottom may be carnal, God's reason for using them is for our sanctification.

Loving our enemies

Jesus therefore puts to us the greatest challenge that ever was. It is a greater challenge to the human spirit than when science put man on the moon. It is, simply, the greatest challenge on earth: to love your enemy. Jesus uses the word *agape*, as Paul would use in 1 Corinthians 13. It is not *eros* (physical or sexual love), nor *philia* (brotherly love). *Agape* is *selfless concern*. It is self-giving love. It is not necessarily affection. You may love a person, and not want to spend a holiday with them. You may love a person and not like them; but you can act unselfishly.

This can be almost overwhelming. The challenge Jesus puts to us is to overwhelm your enemy; not by showing everybody how wrong he or she was – not matching their hatred with yours. The challenge Jesus puts is: overwhelm them by loving them. When you do this you have responded to and achieved the greatest challenge on earth.

We are back to this matter of choice. Love is not what you feel. Forgiving is not doing what comes naturally. It is often said, 'You can't help what you feel.' We therefore ask, is the choice to love someone repressing or denying feelings? No. Repression is almost never a good thing to do. Repressing is playing games with your mind and you may not know you are doing it. Love is a conscious choice to forgive – even if you don't feel like it! Don't wait until you feel like it or you probably never will forgive. Do it because it is right, not because you feel like letting them off the hook. We therefore choose to forgive – or not to forgive.

Nelson Mandela has been asked many times how he emerged from all those years in prison without being bitter. His reply is simple: 'Bitterness only hurts oneself.' The thing is, however, many who are bitter fully realise this, yet they still can't forgive. They know in their heads – rationally – that this bitterness is self-impoverishing. But they keep on doing it, feeling bitter. How did Nelson Mandela make this transition? The answer is in his words to President Bill Clinton: 'If you hate you will give them your heart and mind. Don't give those two things away.'

The paradox in total forgiveness is that it is simultaneous selfishness and unselfishness. It is selfish – in that you like yourself too much to hurt yourself by bitterness. It is unselfish in that you commit yourself to someone never getting punished! You could almost say that total forgiveness is both extreme selfishness and extreme unselfishness. You are looking out for your own interest when you totally forgive, but when you totally set someone free you are taking your hands off once and for all.

The issue then becomes, which will win: overcoming the anger that someone won't get found out or punished – which is doing yourself a favour – or giving in to the bitterness and working day and night for them to get their 'come-uppance'

– which will eat into your very soul and eventually destroy you?

Even the non-Christian faces this. Not a few cases of relief and thrill of totally forgiving – by those who are not Christians – can be told. One forgives in such cases not because that person wants to please God; not because bitterness grieves the Spirit; not because setting people free ensures a greater anointing. One does it because he or she is better off physically and emotionally for forgiving, worse off for not forgiving.

But I write in this book as a Christian, mainly for Christians. This surely leaves all of us without excuse. If therefore a non-Christian can forgive another, how much more should the Christian do it? We are the ones who have been warned by Jesus: 'For if you forgive men when they sin against you, your heavenly Father will also forgive you. But if you do not forgive men their sins, your Father will not forgive your sins' (Matt. 6:14–15). This means that as Christians we have no choice. This means we forfeit fellowship with God and blessing here on earth when we don't forgive. If we have been forgiven of all our sins – and this includes sins we have forgotten about – then how dare we withhold this from others?

Trying to justify our sin

The mistake many of us make is this. We say openly and (seemingly) reasonably, 'I know I am a sinner. I have done some pretty horrible things – but not as bad and horrible as that which they have done to me.' That is a most common line, whether it be rape, child abuse, vicious lying or infidelity. We say, 'I would never rape or murder or physically abuse anybody.' Or we say, 'I may have stolen from Sainsbury's. I may have cheated on my income tax. I may have gossiped a bit. But I would never abuse a child.' We may be among those who say, 'I know what it is to lose my temper. I have been jealous at times. I have coveted someone's success. But I've never done anything so wicked as to be unfaithful to my beloved spouse.'

I understand this. Most of us have to forgive specific wrongs that we ourselves may well never do to another. True. But what we also don't realise at first – and the truth may not be faced for a long time – is the meaning of Jesus' words that those of us who are unjust in that which is least will also be unjust in that which is much (Luke 16:10). Agree or disagree, that is Jesus' doctrine of sin. That is his view of people. The 'little' sins we do that seem relatively harmless (taking a ballpoint pen from the office) only show what else we would do if we knew we would get away with it. The mild flirtation with the opposite sex is but the tip of the iceberg of what we would love to do – if we knew we wouldn't get caught.

The point is this. God not only knows the sins we have committed but the sins we are capable of. He knows our hearts. He sees what is deep down inside that we may not be willing to face. Our self-righteousness and personal sense of decency often camouflage the evil that is deep within. When Jesus' blood cleanses us from all *sin* (1 John 1:7), that means being forgiven for what is there that we hadn't been aware of. The truth is, given the right circumstances, pressure, temptation, places and timing, *any* of us can match the evil (or its equivalent in God's sight) we ourselves have to forgive. If we deny this it is because we don't agree with what the Bible says about men and women of any colour, whatever culture, education or background.

And yet agreeing with the Bible doesn't make it easy. We are still indignant that this person – who knows the truth and should have known better – could carry out this deed, or hurt us like that. But the Bible is saying that we too are either (1) guilty of a different sin which is just as heinous in God's eyes, or (2) capable of a sin just as bad in God's eyes, or (3) we may yet fall into such a sin as they did – or worse. Do be careful here. Not forgiving not only leads to deeper bitterness but, as we have already seen, the capability of enacting a wrong that is worse than we ever dreamed of doing. God *could* judge us by allowing us eventually to fall into the exact same sin that we are required to forgive – should we dig our heels in and remain recalcitrant. I have certainly seen it happen. I know for a fact of people who were indignant over a particular kind of conduct who, later, did the very thing they criticised. This is why Jesus said, 'Do not judge, or you too will be judged' (Matt. 7:1).

God none the less gives us motives for doing the right thing by appealing to our self-interest. He doesn't have to; he could say, 'Just do it because I say so and because it is right.' He could, but he doesn't. He could have said, 'You have robbed God by withholding tithes. Start doing it because this is my Law.' He could have said that, but he didn't. He said, ' "Bring the whole tithe into the storehouse, that there may be food in my house. Test me in this," says the LORD Almighty, "and see if I will not throw open the floodgates of heaven and pour out so much blessing that you will not have room enough for it" ' (Mal. 3:10). In the same way, God appeals to us to do what is commanded and right – but in such a way as to encourage us to obey.

The pragmatic reasons for forgiving

What are the pragmatic reasons for forgiving?

1 Consider the consequences if you do forgive

'Release them and you will be released,' Josif Tson said to me. What I didn't think I *could* do, I did do. Josif was right. I felt released inside. The bondage wasn't worth it. The absence of seeing Jesus' face wasn't worth it. The lack of peace wasn't worth it. But getting that old peace back – I had forgotten what it was like – was worth it all. God is a jealous God and won't let us enjoy this inner blissful peace if we have an unforgiving spirit.

I remember when I first became aware that the old peace was gone. It was in August 1956. Less than a year before that I had what I like to call my own Damascus Road experience, when driving in my car from Palmer to Nashville, Tennessee. The Lord Jesus Christ blessed me with such peace that I could not describe it were I Shakespeare, Wordsworth and Shelley rolled into one. The peace was simply indescribable. But in August 1956 I lost my temper with my father. He accused me of recanting on what I'd been brought up to believe and said I was utterly out of God's will. I completely 'lost it', as they say. I shouldn't have, but I did. I felt so awful afterwards. If only I could have asked him to forgive me for losing my temper (I didn't) and if only I had forgiven him for his well-meaning but untrue words (I didn't). Instead I determined to spend the next few years vindicating myself. I might wish that a Josif Tson had come alongside me at that time and warned me of the consequences of my bitterness. If only. All I know is, it was a long time before I found the key to the way back to peace.

That's strange, isn't it? Here we have the plain words of Jesus in the Lord's Prayer, not to mention all the words of Jesus and the rest of the New Testament. And I tried everything from tithing, double tithing, praying two hours a day, walking forward in a service any time I felt the urge, having some person lay hands on me and other things. All I needed to do was to forgive my father – and an ever-increasing number of people who subsequently questioned me and the direction of my life.

If this book is tailor-made for you (because you are struggling to forgive and to overcome bitterness), consider the inner peace and the clear thinking that is closer than your fingertips, closer than the air you breathe. It is near you, even in your heart. Forgive them. Release them. Do it in your heart. Refuse those imaginary conversations that rob you of time and sleep. Think pleasant thoughts. 'Finally, brothers, whatever is true, whatever is noble, whatever is right, whatever is pure, whatever is lovely, whatever is admirable – if anything is excellent or praiseworthy – think about such things' (Phil. 4:8). If you must have imaginary conversations, imagine refusing to tell what you know, and instead set that person free and think about putting them at ease.

What motivation Stephen may have had to attain to such a zenith of spirituality as he achieved, I don't know. I doubt that God said, 'Forgive your enemies and your example will play a part in the conversion of Saul of Tarsus.' All I know is, when Stephen was in immense pain from their stoning him and he caved in physically such that he eventually died, he managed to utter, 'Lord, do not hold this sin against them' (Acts 7:60). Saul witnessed the whole thing and he never forgot it. So with us. 'As it is written: "No eye has seen, no ear has heard, no mind has conceived what God has prepared for those who love him" ' (1 Cor. 2:9). Who knows how God will use you if you – once for all – set someone free and never look back.

2 Consider the consequences if you don't forgive

Jesus put this very strongly indeed: 'But if you do not forgive men their sins, your Father will not forgive your sins' (Matt. 6:15). That doesn't mean you won't be guided or looked after. God still guided and looked after me. But now I realise why I lost so much that I had once had. Great though God's plans for me may have been, he didn't bend the rules for me. He allowed me to get deep into debt and suffer the humiliation of having to be out of the full-time preaching ministry; I peddled vacuum cleaners as a door-to-door sales-man for years, living under a cloud whereby nobody believed in me, and having my godly father believe all he feared most concerning me.

Whether I hurt my health in all this, I can't say. But in some cases the refusal to forgive leads to countless physical ailments. Lack of forgiveness is ageing; it puts lines on faces before they should come. In some cases it means sleeplessness.

Having to forgive my father is *not* what was at hand when I had my aforementioned encounter with Josif Tson, for my friendship with Josif came many years later. But what is true is this. Not forgiving my father made it easy and natural to be bitter later. The person who became like a substitute father (I turned to someone else for approval) hurt me even more than my father had – and the bitterness towards him was a thousand times worse. But I felt no conviction that this was wrong. Neither did God manifest himself in any great power. I forfeited anointing that could have been mine, though.

The consequences of an unforgiving spirit add up to one

thing: the bitterness isn't worth it. The devil does not want you to forgive others; he loves it when you are bitter. This way he has access to you. He therefore will put up what appear to be good reasons for wanting your adversary to be punished – and by you if at all possible. Those imaginary conversations are inspired by him, by the way. He wants to rob you of time and energy and joy. You can expect obstacles to be put in your way if you try to forgive. They will seem 'providential' – excuses why you are the exception to the rule. Never forget that when Jonah decided to run from God and head for Tarshish he found (providentially!) a ship that was going there (Jonah 1:3); it seemed at the time that God was behind his decision. So you too will find ways and reasons why you need not forgive, but the consequences of this are disastrous.

Since forgiveness is a choice, what is the next step? If we are persuaded that it is right and we have decided to do it (and not look back), what next? The answer has already been given in Chapter 2, but I will restate the reasons here.

Steps in totally forgiving others

1 Make the deliberate and irrevocable choice not to tell anybody what they did

(As I said above, you may need to do this for therapeutic reasons, but only to one person who in their turn will never reveal your own heart.) Jesus also said that the one who is faithful in the least thing is faithful also in much, and this is the first thing. Do not mention it; refuse to tell anybody.

This isn't necessarily easy sometimes, but when our motive is to hurt another person by telling on them, there is sin on our part. So do not tell it at all or in part; keep it quiet.

2 Be pleasant to them should you be around them

Do not throw anything up; do not say or do anything that would make them anxious. Put them at their ease.

This can be hard to do, certainly harder than the first step. It is we who are afraid when we can't forgive. When we pass our fear to them it is utterly the opposite of what Jesus would do. He would say, 'Fear not.' Josif Tson says that there are 366 statements of 'Do not fear' (or the equivalent) in the Bible; 'One for every day of the year and one for leap year!' he says. God doesn't want us to fear; we must not do or say anything to cause others to fear. Be nice. Put them at ease. That is what Jesus did when he turned up after his resurrection to ten disciples behind closed doors (John 20:19).

3 If conversation ensues, say that which would set them free from guilt

Guilt is most painful, and we can easily punish people by sending them on a 'guilt trip'. Never do that. Remember that Jesus doesn't want us to feel guilty. When we are going to be Jesus to another, then we will not want them to be angry with themselves.

This is a hard one. We get some satisfaction when we think they feel really, really bad. That defuses us and eases our anger somewhat. But if we want to be valiant and utterly magnanimous – thus showing true godliness – we will say whatever is the equivalent of Joseph's words, 'Do not be angry with yourselves' (Gen. 45:5). He would not allow his brothers to feel guilty and this is a choice we must make. It's hard, but it is what *we* would want if things were reversed and we needed forgiveness. 'Do to others as you would have them do to you' (Luke 6:31).

4 Let them feel good about themselves

Not only does this mean *never* reminding them of their wrong and your hurt, but it means helping them through any guilt they may have. This can be done without any reference to what they did. If it is not in the open, as with Joseph's situation, that is of course different; he let his brothers save face by showing God's sovereign strategy in their sin. But in many cases you will not be able to talk about anything specifically. You can still let them save face because you know that they know what they did.

You therefore must behave as though you don't even think they did anything wrong! That is hard for all of us, but it must be done. Say whatever you can (as long as it is true) that will give that person a sense of dignity. That is the point of Galatians 6:1: 'Brothers, if someone is caught in a sin, you who are spiritual should restore him gently. But watch yourself, or you also may be tempted.' As long as there is a trace of self-righteousness and pointing the finger, your attempt at total forgiveness will backfire.

The best way to let another save face is to feel and show your own vulnerability – that you would have done what they did had you been them and been where they were at the time. When you respect them by showing you are a sinner great as any and worse than many – which is true – it lets them feel better. And keep some dignity. God does that with us.

5 Protect them from their greatest fear

If you are aware of some deep, dark secret and fear they have, they will probably know that you know. If they can tell by your graciousness that their secret will never be revealed – ever – to anyone, they will be relieved. You only tell them when you know they know what you know, and you are convinced this would make them feel better. If by reminding them it would obviously not make them feel better, don't even come close!

It will be recalled that Joseph knew his brothers' greatest fear was that their father Jacob would learn the truth of their evil deed. Joseph never mentioned this directly but suggested they speak to Jacob in such a way that they wouldn't have to tell him after all (see Gen. 45:9–13). It must have given the brothers incalculable relief to know that they were not obliged to tell Jacob. But that is what total forgiveness is all about: setting people free.

6 Keep it up today, tomorrow, this year and next

As we have said, total forgiveness is a life-long commitment. Some days will be easier than others. There will come a time when you think you are completely over it and have won a total victory – only to find the very next day Satan reminds you of what they did and the utter injustice that they will be unpunished and never exposed. The temptation to bitterness will emerge. After all, we're not perfect! If we say we have no sin – that we are incapable of the same old bitterness – we are deceived (1 John 1:8).

This is exactly why I read Luke 6:37 every day: 'Do not judge, and you will not be judged. Do not condemn, and you will not be condemned. Forgive, and you will be forgiven.' All commitments to forgive need renewal. In my case, daily. I am not telling you that this is what *you* must do, but be warned: the devil is cunning. He will come through the back door unexpectedly and try to upset you for forgiving. When you forgave your enemy you then and there removed that open invitation to the devil to get inside. Satan's favourite rationale is bitterness – he therefore will keep trying to get back into your thought life.

Whether it be Luke 6:37 or another way forward in your case – even if you aren't required to keep it up each day – I can tell you right now that it is only a matter of time before your commitment to forgive will need to be renewed.

7 Pray for them

'But I tell you: Love your enemies and pray for those who persecute you' (Matt. 5:44). When you do this from the heart – praying for their being blessed and off the hook – you're there. It is not a perfunctory prayer, not a 'We commit them to you' prayer, and certainly not a 'O God, please deal with them' prayer. It is praying that God will forgive them – that is, *overlook* what they have done and bless and prosper them as though they'd never sinned at all.

But as John Calvin said, doing this is 'exceedingly difficult'. As Chrysostom (*c.* 344–407) said, it is the very highest summit of self-control. 'Better a patient man than a warrior, a man who controls his temper than one who takes a city' (Prov. 16:32).

Praying for one who has hurt you or let you down is the greatest challenge of all, for three reasons: (1) you take a route utterly against the flesh; (2) nobody will ever know you are doing it, and (3) your heart could break when God answers that prayer and truly blesses them as if they'd never sinned.

And yet Jesus' word to pray for such people is not a polite suggestion; it is a command – and one that may seem so outrageous that you want to dismiss it out of hand. Some see it as a lofty but unrealistic goal.

I remember a church leader turning to me to pray about his son-in-law who had been unfaithful to the leader's daughter. He said to me that his own prayer was only this: that God would 'deal' with this man. 'That is where I have come to,' he said to me, 'that God will deal with him.' I understood what he meant; I felt for him. I find what people do to our own offspring the hardest things to forgive. I therefore understood what he was feeling. A few days later it was reported that this man's son-in-law had been in a serious accident. This same church leader was on the phone, glad that the accident had happened. Now in this particular case there was nothing sinister in this euphoria. He simply hoped that the accident would wake up this son-in-law to put his marriage back together. It was so understandable.

But that is not what Jesus means. He is commanding us to pray that our enemy will be *blessed*. If, however, you should pray that they will be cursed or punished instead of being blessed, just remember that is how your enemy possibly feels about you. After all, have *you* ever been someone's enemy? Have *you* ever done something that brought a fellow Christian to tears and brokenness? If so, how would you like that person to pray for *you*? That God will deal with *you*? That God will cause *you* to have an accident? Yet how would it make you feel if they prayed that you would be blessed and let off the hook and that you would prosper as if you'd never sinned? Would you not like that? 'Do to others as you would have them do to you' (Luke 6:31).

Jesus wants a sincere prayer from us. It is like signing your name to a document, having it witnessed and never looking back. You are not allowed to tell the world: 'Guess what I did? I have actually prayed for my unfaithful spouse to be blessed.' No. It is quiet. Only the angels witness it, but it makes God very happy.

After all, every parent wants their children to get on with

one another. No parent likes it when one child comes and squeals on the other and demands that they be punished. The poor parent is put on the spot. What gladdens the heart of every parent is when there is love and forgiveness and you aren't put on the spot to have to take sides and punish anybody. That is what we do for God when we ask that he bless and not curse. He told us to pray for our enemies, 'that you may be sons of your Father in heaven. He causes his sun to rise on the evil and the good, and sends rain on the righteous and the unrighteous' (Matt. 5:45).

The five stages in praying for our enemies

There are five stages, or levels, of praying for one's enemy:

Duty. That's the first level, and there is nothing wrong with that. It is obedience, even if you are doing it because you feel you have to.

Debt. This is when you are so conscious of what you have been forgiven that you cannot but pray for your enemy. You don't want God to spill the beans on you, so you pray that they too will be spared.

Desire. It is what you really want. Not that you felt this way at first; it began as duty. But now you have reached the stage where you actually want to pray for those who have hurt you.

Delight. This is taking desire a step further. It is when you love doing it! You get your joy from knowing that God knows. You know that this is pleasing to him. And not far from your mind is the fact that praying in this manner means a greater anointing and reward in heaven (Matt. 5:12).

Durability. This means that what you took on as a life-long commitment becomes a lifestyle. The thought of turning back or praying in a different way is out of the question. It has become a habit and it no longer seems like something extraordinary.

As Jackie Pullinger said, 'To the spiritual person the supernatural seems natural.' What began as a duty and seemed insurmountable is now almost second nature.

All this is in secret. Behind the scenes. Only the angels know. It is quiet intercession. You aren't allowed to get your reward or applause from people who may think, 'Oh isn't that lovely that you should pray for your enemy like that.' No. It is a secret that must never be told. Enter into your place of prayer and shut the door behind you. 'Then your Father, who sees what is done in secret, will reward you' (Matt. 6:4).

There are several consequences of praying for your enemy or the person who has disappointed you. The obvious consequence is that reward in heaven. It may be manifested in one of two ways or both: (1) blessing and greater anointing on earth – which comes from heaven of course (Jesus didn't necessarily say we had to wait until we die); (2) that great reward when we get to heaven. That is the guaranteed consequence of praying like this.

Be warned of another consequence – God may answer your prayer! 'Oh no!' you may say, 'I only prayed it because I was being obedient. Surely God would not actually hear my prayer and literally bless and prosper that wicked person?' Well, he may indeed answer that prayer. Will you still pray it?

By the way, let us assume you have hurt somebody. If they prayed for your prosperity, you wouldn't object, would you? How do you know this hasn't happened? How do you know that your own sense of blessing and fulfilment is not the answer to another's prayer on your behalf but who was really hurt by you? You may say, 'They would never pray for me like that.' Perhaps. But the very fact that you are blessed and yet have caused hurt in someone is proof that God hasn't chosen to throw the book at you yet. Be thankful for just that, and pray that it may continue by asking God to show mercy on them – if only that you may be the continued beneficiary of mercy.

Yes, God may answer that prayer. He answered Jesus' prayer for forgiveness of his tormentors at Calvary (Luke 23:34) and 3,000 were converted in one day (Acts 2:41). He answered Moses' prayer and a whole nation was spared (Num. 14:19).

Another surprising consequence of your prayer is that, just maybe, your enemy may become your friend. Today's enemy may be tomorrow's friend. That is what God did to us: 'That God was reconciling the world to himself in Christ, not counting men's sins against them. And he has committed to us the message of reconciliation' (2 Cor. 5:19). You too may well win your enemy over by loving them and praying for them. 'I don't want this person as a friend,' you may say. That's OK. We saw earlier that total forgiveness does not always mean reconciliation. Do not feel guilty if you don't want to become close friends, but in some cases this has happened. And if there is a reconciliation or a coming together in friendship, that person may say to you, 'You were brilliant the whole time. You were loving and caring, never vindictive.' A rule of thumb: treat your enemy now the way you will be glad you did should you become good friends.

The greatest consequence of all, however, is just knowing

that you have pleased God. I want to be like Enoch who had this testimony: he pleased God (Heb. 11:5). Nothing pleases God as much as our loving and praying for our enemies. It is significant that Job's troubles stopped and his captivity turned when he prayed for those friends who were his real persecutors and tormentors during his suffering. 'After Job had prayed for his friends, the LORD made him prosperous again and gave him twice as much as he had before' (Job 42:10).

Doing this is, of course, our duty – but it eventually becomes a delight. If you hate, you will give your enemy your heart and mind. As Nelson Mandela said, don't give those two things away.

Conclusion

Margaret Moss, whose husband Norman was the Minster of Queen's Road Baptist Church in Wimbledon, has given me permission to share the following two stories. I learned of them from her because I asked the Mosses if they had seen anybody healed lately. She gave two recent examples and both, as it happens, pertained to the theme of this book.

The first concerned a woman who had been in a car accident twenty-two years before. For all these years, her neck had given her constant pain, and she had to forfeit her driving licence because she could not move her head in either direction – not even being able to look into the rear view mirror. Margaret asked her if she had ever prayed for the driver of the car who had caused the accident. 'No,' she replied. 'I suggested that she pray for him,' Margaret said. 'I forgive him,' the lady then prayed. 'Now bless him,' Margaret suggested. The woman began to bless this man. 'The pain went,' said Margaret. The next morning the woman could move her neck for the first time in twenty-two years. That was over a year ago and the healing has continued.

The second account involved a lady in her forties whose father had severely abused her. This lady claimed that she had said to the Lord, 'I forgive him' – again and again. But despite praying this she had continued in 'heaviness of spirit', Margaret told me. 'I then suggested that she began blessing her father as well as saying she forgave him,' she said. 'The moment she said, "I bless my father", she went ballistic!' The heaviness completely went! The last time Margaret saw this lady she said that the spirit of heaviness had still gone and the lady added, 'Now my life has completely changed.'

As to the need in these two cases for the prayer of blessing to be offered as well as forgiveness before they were released, I can only conclude that forgiveness is not *total* forgiveness until we bless our enemies – and pray for them to be blessed. Forgiving them is a major step; *totally* forgiving them has fully set in when we set God free, as it were, to bless them. For when we ask God to forgive them, and mean it, he is going to overlook their wrong as though it never happened – which allows them to be blessed.

Yet we are the *first* to be blessed, and I would suspect also that those who totally forgive are blessed the most.

In the Introduction to this book we noted how the teaching and carrying out of forgiveness has been recognised as valid and therapeutic even outside the realm of the Christian faith. You will recall the *Daily Express* article about the course in Leeds. The reason for this course in Leeds, which was paid for by a £120,000 grant from the John Templeton Foundation, was apparently because forgiving can be good for your health. Holding a grudge, it is said, leads to illnesses ranging from common colds to heart disease because of all the stored-up anger and stress. Dr Sandi Mann, a psychologist at the

University of Central Lancashire, believes that there is a strong link between our emotions and our immune system. All this goes to demonstrate the benefits of forgiving people – even if someone is not motivated by Jesus and the New Testament! Indeed, here are ten steps to freedom, as found in the *Daily Express*'s article:

1 Stop excusing, pardoning or rationalising.
2 Pinpoint the actions that have hurt you.
3 Spend time thinking of ways in which your life would be more satisfying if you could let go of your grievances.
4 Try replacing angry thoughts about the 'badness' of the perpetrator with thoughts about how the offender is also a human being who is vulnerable to harm.
5 Identify yourself with the offender's probable state of mind. Understand the perpetrator's history while not condoning his or her actions.
6 Spend some time developing greater compassion towards the perpetrator.
7 Become more aware that you have needed other people's forgiveness in the past.
8 Make a heart-felt resolution not to pass on one's own pain.
9 Spend time appreciating the sense of purpose and direction that comes after steps 1 to 8.
10 Enjoy the sense of emotional relief that comes when the burden of a grudge has melted away. Enjoy also the feeling of goodwill and mercy you have shown.

There is a phrase in the Epistle to the Hebrews, 'How much more' (Heb. 9:14; 10:29). The point there is that if certain things were true under the Mosaic Law, *how much more* is promised now that Christ has come and fulfilled the Law?

It seems to me therefore that if the secular world is catching on to the teachings of Jesus – even if not acknowledging him or the Holy Spirit – and deriving benefit, how much more should Christians experience this? In other words, if non-Christians can find peace because it is better for their health, how much more should you and I – who want to please God and honour the Holy Spirit – grasp this teaching with all our hearts? It surely leaves us all without excuse.

The most profound thing I ever heard Joni Eareckson Tada say is this: 'I am a Christian not because of what it does for me but because it is true.' We therefore should believe Christ's teaching because it is true.

But it also works. Let the past be past – at last!